MANCHESTER UNITED®

OFFICIAL MEMBERS' HISTORY BOOK

The Story of the World's Greatest Football Club

First published in 2004

Published, manufactured and distributed by
Carlton Books Limited
20 Mortimer Street
London W1T 3JW

Copyright © Manchester United plc 2004
Design and text copyright © Carlton Books Limited 2004

Features excerpts from *The Official Manchester United Illustrated History*

A CIP catalogue record of this book is available from the British Library

ISBN 0 233 00113 1

Contributors: Justyn Barnes, Adam Bostock, Cliff Butler,
Aubrey Ganguly, Graham McColl and Mark Wylie

Edited by: Aubergine

Art Director: David Hicks

Production: Lisa French

Printed in Belgium

INTRODUCTION

Today's Manchester United players are accustomed to walking out in front of 67,000-plus crowds at Old Trafford to take on the cream of European football.

With them they carry the weight of our club's extraordinary history. From humble beginnings as a works team playing beside a railway, through the tragedy of Munich to an unprecedented Treble triumph, it has taken the passion, dedication and skill of many people to reach the summit of club football.

Let's relive the remarkable story of the club we all love...

NEWTON HEATH (L.Y.R.)
Cricket and Football Club.

ESTABLISHED 1878.

SEASON 1882-1883.

President:
F. ATTOCK, Esq.

Vice-Presidents:
MR. W. LORD. | MR. T. R. GORST.

Committee:
MR. A. SHAW. | MR. C. CHORLTON.
MR. C. LATHAM. | MR. G. SMITH.
MR. J. RIGBY.

Captain:
MR. E. THOMAS.

Vice-Captain:
MR. J. CRAMPHORN.

Hon. Secretary:
MR. E. HOLE, 493, OLDHAM ROAD,
NEWTON HEATH.

CHAPTER ONE
GETTING ON TRACK

Long before Manchester United became one of the most famous football clubs in the world, they were a works team, created on the other side of the city along the railway lines of the Lancashire and Yorkshire Railway at Newton Heath...

In the second half of the nineteenth century, Manchester was thriving, full of mills, factories and workshops and home to over 400,000 people – a city rapidly expanding and cementing its place as the cotton cloth capital of the world. Even in 1835, a French visitor described it thus:

The footsteps of a busy crowd, the crunching wheels of machinery, the shriek of steam from boilers, the regular beat of the looms, the heavy rumble of carts, these are the noises from which you can never escape in the sombre half-light of these streets.
Journeys to England and Ireland by A. de Tocqueville

By the 1870s, there was very little heath left in Newton Heath, an area that had been mainly countryside only 20 years before. The Lancashire and Yorkshire Railway Company had chosen Newton Heath for one of its depots and for a carriage and wagon works. It was at this carriage and wagon works that the team that would become Manchester United was formed.

In common with many other large Victorian employers, the Lancashire and Yorkshire Railway took an interest in the social lives of its employees, probably in an attempt to steer them away from the temptations of alcohol. To this end, the company had organized "classes of improvement". The Dining Room Committee at the works was responsible for these, and swiftly took over the supervision of a proposed cricket and football club, one of a number of sports clubs that were set up by the workmen. The new club, founded in 1878, was called Newton Heath (Lancashire and Yorkshire Railway) Cricket & Football Club.

Cricket and rugby were generally the preferred sports around Manchester, but football was slowly gaining a toehold in the city. A patch of land was found adjacent to the works on North Road and cricketers and footballers shared this ground throughout the year. Never the best of pitches, it was dogged by drainage problems in the winter and the ground became renowned as a mud bath.

Despite the poor pitch, which must have caused at least as many problems for the cricketers, this was to be the home of Newton Heath (L & Y R) Cricket & Football Club into the 1890s. There were no changing facilities whatsoever in those early years, the players having to resort to using a public house on Oldham Road. This pub, The Three Crowns, was over half a mile from the ground, a distance that must have seemed at least twice as far after a bruising match on the terrible pitch. Later the Shears Hotel, also on Oldham Road, served as changing rooms and unofficial club headquarters before an office was rented at 33 Oldham Road.

In these early days football was seldom reported on, even in the many local newspapers. It is likely that the men from Newton Heath played matches against fellow workers at the depot, for instance the engine

1878	1878	1880
Newton Heath (Lancashire and Yorkshire Railway) Football Club is formed. The club's initial home is North End.	Club President F. Attock gathers notable figures as vice-presidents, including the future British Prime Minister A.J. Balfour.	The club nickname 'The Heathens' comes into prominent usage as Newton Heath record a series of victories over local rival football teams.

drivers who went on to form a team of their own, Newton Heath Loco(motive). As a company-approved activity, matches between departments and against other depots would have been the most likely fixtures. Green and gold, the colours of the Lancashire and Yorkshire Railway, were chosen as the club colours and soon these green and gold halved shirts became well known around the Manchester area.

The President of the club was Mr F. Attock, the superintendent of the carriage and wagon works. Around him he gathered some of the most notable men of the day as vice-presidents. These included three local MPs – A.J. Balfour (who went on to become Prime Minister in the 1890s), C.E. Schwann and Sir James Ferguson – and C.P. Scott, the editor of the *Manchester Guardian*.

By the early 1880s, Newton Heath were not only challenging other teams from both their own and other railway companies' depots, but were also venturing further afield. Teams such as Manchester Arcadians, Hurst and West Gorton became familiar opponents in the multitude of friendly matches arranged throughout the season. Games against the longer-established teams of Lancashire were, if truth be told, an aspiration. Newton Heath were one of the best teams in Manchester, but they were no match for even the reserve sides of clubs such as Bolton Wanderers. Two 6–0 defeats against the Trotters reserves confirmed the Heathens' place in the game. But visits to places as far away as St Helens, Southport and Crewe became a reality as the club looked further than its local patch.

Tempted away from a continual round of friendly matches, Newton Heath entered the Lancashire Cup in the 1883/84 season, but crashed out 7–2 in the first round to the FA Cup holders, Blackburn Olympic. The club evidently still had a fair amount of progress to make before it could reasonably tackle the Lancashire clubs. However, impressed by the performance of Newton Heath's captain, Sam Black, Blackburn Olympic tried to entice him

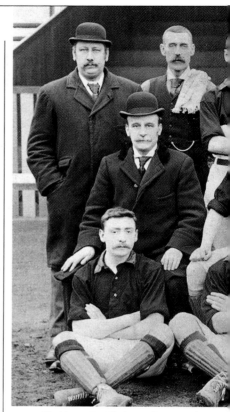

over to Blackburn. But Black was determined to remain a Heathen, which he did until he eventually returned to his hometown and joined Burton Wanderers.

The foundation of the Manchester Cup for 1884/85 gave Newton Heath a local challenge and the opportunity to win a trophy. They stormed through to the final where, before a crowd of 4,000 spectators, they met old rivals Hurst from nearby Ashton-under-Lyne. Despite losing just one match throughout the season, a 3–0 defeat left the Heathens licking their wounds, but it was the start of a purple patch for the club in the Manchester Cup. In its first nine seasons, Newton Heath were finalists on no less than eight occasions, going on to win it in 1886, 1888, 1889, 1890 and 1893. The 1886 success brought Newton Heath their

1882
Newton Heath begin travelling further afield to play matches. St Helens, Southport and Crewe are among the destinations.

1883
The Heathens enter the Lancashire Cup but exit in the first round following a 7–2 thrashing from Blackburn Olympic.

1883
Club captain Sam Black turns down an offer to leave Newton Heath and join Blackburn Olympic.

Newton Heath at Bank Street, wearing their green shirts with gold trim, and with shinguards outside their socks.

first-ever trophy, although the controversial 2–1 victory over Manchester FC on 3 April provoked many arguments in the bars of East Manchester. The Heathens' winning goal was claimed by Manchester to be both offside and a handball.

The Heathens' success did not go unnoticed. Four players won caps as representatives of Manchester District in March 1884. The majority of the players still worked at the wagon works and most lived close by. However, all was not as it seemed. The possibility of gaining a job working on the railway became a major incentive for players from further afield. Professionalism was still illegal, but many of the prominent Lancashire clubs were finding success by adding some talented Scottish players to their ranks. These players were primarily in Lancashire for the football, but were found jobs to keep up the pretence of amateurism. Newton Heath employed similar tactics and in the mid-1880s an influx of Welshmen arrived, with jobs being found for them at the works. Newton Heath were not a wealthy club, despite having the backing of the Lancashire and Yorkshire Railway Company. It was essentially still a works team, far removed from the semi-professional elite of Lancashire with their wealthy backers. However, the Welsh influx brought some established international players – Jack Powell, from Bolton Wanderers, Joe Davies, Tom Burke, Jack Owens and brothers Jack and Roger Doughty.

The 1886/87 season saw Newton Heath enter the FA Cup for the first time, one of the

1884
The Manchester Cup is founded. Newton Heath reach the first-ever final but are defeated 3–0 by local rivals Hurst.

1884
Four Newton Heath players win caps as representatives of Manchester District.

1886
Newton Heath enter the FA Cup for the first time, but go out in the first round to Fleetwood Rangers after refusing to play extra-time following a 2–2 draw.

few clubs from the Manchester area to do so. They drew Fleetwood Rangers in the first round. Two Jack Doughty goals earned a 2–2 draw but, asked to play extra-time, Newton Heath refused and the referee awarded victory to Fleetwood Rangers. It was a sorry end to the Heathens' first attempt to win the FA Cup.

It was in August 1887 that Pat O'Donnell famously walked from Glasgow to Newton Heath in search of a job. He won both a job at the carriage works and, soon after, a place in the team. The *Manchester Evening News* noted the composition of the Newton Heath team on 1 October 1887:

…Burke, Davies, Powell, Owen and Doughty are all Welshmen, while Tait is a Scotchman and O'Donnell, Irish; in fact with the exception of Wright, we do not recognize a local man in the team.

Professionalism was making an impact, but in the 1887/88 season, Newton Heath were known to have just two professional players: goalkeeper Tom Hay and full-back Jack Powell. This was far fewer than the Lancashire elite, who were pressing for the formation of a league system. Newton Heath were still the most successful club in the Manchester area and hoped for an invitation to join the elite. However, they were rejected by the Football League. They responded by joining other similarly rejected clubs in setting up their own competition – the Football Combination. Unfortunately, this competition was not as well thought through as the Football League and lasted just one season. The member clubs continued to play round after round of friendly matches. Newton Heath found themselves playing as many friendlies as before, even if one was against international opposition – they lost 2–0 to a Canadian XI.

The problems of the Football Combination were quickly realized and acted upon. For the

Caesar Jenkyns

following season, a new competition emerged, the Football Alliance. Newton Heath struggled to find any consistency, finishing in the bottom half of the table. They entered the FA Cup but again lasted a solitary round. Up against the holders and league champions, the Invincibles of Preston North End, Newton Heath crashed out, losing 6–1.

Friendlies were still a major part of Newton Heath's season despite their Football Alliance fixtures. Harsh economic reality made it a necessity despite the obvious effects that too many matches had on the stamina of their players over the season: friendlies against local opposition often attracted far higher crowds than the Alliance fixtures. Newton Heath had never been a rich club and without a major wealthy financial backer these extra costs forced them to walk a financial tightrope each season.

Desperate to gain entry to the Football League, Newton Heath made an annual application for membership, but season after season they were rejected. Eager to show the Football League their status as the best club in Manchester, in 1891 the committee members went ahead with the construction of two new stands at North Road, able to hold over 2,000 supporters.

A concerted effort was made to win the Alliance as the club's committee members belatedly woke up to the thought that only success would gain the club access to the Football League. For once things ran relatively smoothly and Newton Heath finished runners-up in the Football Alliance. At the same time, the Football League announced its expansion to include a bigger First Division and a new Second Division. For Newton Heath fans, this was a dream come true – league football, in fact First Division football.

The promise of league football drastically altered the club. All connections with the

1886 The Manchester Cup provides Newton Heath with their first-ever trophy. They repeat the success in 1888, 1889, 1890 and 1893.	**1887** Newton Heath's second entry into the FA Cup ends in a first round exit again – this time at the hands of Preston North End.	**1892** A new limited company, Newton Heath FC is formed, no longer with any connection to the Lancashire and Yorkshire Railway.

railway company were finally severed and, in 1892, a new limited company, Newton Heath FC, was formed. Newton Heath's expenses took a sharp rise and a club secretary was employed for the first time – Alf Albut, signed from Aston Villa. The railway company responded to the formation of the new company by raising the rent of the North Road ground. Furthermore, the bonus of concessionary railway travel vanished. The share floatation was a great disappointment. Share capital in the form of 2,000 £1 shares was promised but not realized.

Centre-forward Bob Donaldson kicked off in the club's first league match, a baptism of fire against Blackburn Rovers at Ewood Park. Rovers quickly went on the attack, rushing into a 3–0 lead. The position looked desperate for the newcomers, but Donaldson scored Newton Heath's first-ever league goal and Coupar added a second to make the half-time score 3–2 to the Rovers. Both teams added a goal in the second half and Newton Heath were far from disgraced against one of the most famous clubs in the country.

However, league football was of too high a standard for Newton Heath, and despite a small number of fine victories and Bob Donaldson's 16 goals, the team ended the season at the bottom of the table. Strangely enough, Newton Heath's first-ever league victory was against Wolverhampton Wanderers, who in their FA Cup-winning season went down to a 10–1 defeat. This is still a record league victory for Manchester United.

The Heathens had a chance to save their First Division status. At the end of the season, Test matches were played, precursors of the present-day play-offs. The top teams in the Second Division took on the bottom teams in the First and Newton Heath were too strong for the Second Division champions, Small Heath – a 1–1 draw and a 5–2 victory meant that the club stayed up.

In the close season there was further trauma at the club. An eviction notice was served on their North Road ground. There were several possible reasons – complaints from the cricketers, who still played at the ground in the summer, and Newton Heath's practice of charging spectators for admission. By charging for admission, Newton Heath hoped to cover their greatly increased costs, but this, it was alleged, broke the terms of their lease on the ground. Rented from Manchester cathedral by the railway company for the use of all their employees, the fact that the footballers had exclusive use of the ground in the winter gave the railway company an excuse for eviction. Newton Heath were ordered to quit before the start of the next football season.

The severing of links with the railway company probably just hastened the club's move to a new ground. Ordered to leave North Road as they had found it or leave behind their expensive and relatively new stands, the club directors had little option but to leave the stands. Receiving under £100 for them, Newton Heath FC immediately found itself out of pocket.

A new ground had to be found, and quickly. For the club secretary and directors, the summer of 1893 was occupied by the search. The ground had to be ready to receive Burnley in the first home league match of the season. Initial enquiries to the cathedral authorities proved fruitless, but after a thorough search, a new ground was finally found towards the end of June. It was in Bank Street, Clayton, three miles from Newton Heath and their supporters. A rental agreement was quickly drawn up with the Bradford and Clayton Athletic Company.

The new tenants worked hard throughout the summer to get the ground ready for the football crowds. There was already a stand along one side of the pitch and another behind one of the goals. To increase capacity, a new cinder terrace was built behind the other goal.

Some 7,000 spectators saw Burnley kick off in the first league match at the ground. Newton Heath were soon behind and, with the wind behind them, Burnley added a second. The Heathens kept pressurizing and by half-time, goals from Donaldson and Farman

1892
Newton Heath are, after three previously denied applications, finally accepted into the Football League.

1893
The Heathens first league season ends with the club finishing bottom of the table, having conceded 85 goals and gained just 18 points.

1893
Newton Heath retain their place in the First Division following a play-off victory against Small Heath (later to become Birmingham City).

MANCHESTER UNITED **OFFICIAL MEMBERS' HISTORY BOOK**   11

had brought the scores level. A late penalty from Farman gave Newton Heath the lead and a winning start at Bank Street.

The location of Newton Heath's new ground, close to a number of chemical works, gave some visiting fans the excuse that the Heathens players must be used to the foul and toxic smells and therefore gained an extra advantage. It was even alleged that the chimneys belched forth more fumes when Newton Heath were losing in an attempt to put off the opposition!

Despite their winning start to the 1893/94 campaign, Newton Heath were soon in difficulties. The club's directors took exception to an article that was published in the *Birmingham Daily Gazette* on 14 October 1893 after a 4–1 victory over West Bromwich Albion:

It wasn't football, it was simple brutality and if these are the tactics Newton Heath are compelled to adopt to win their matches, the sooner the Football Association deal severely with them the better it will be for the game generally.

The directors sued the newspaper for libel. The case was won, but feelings of victory were short-lived as the judge delivered his verdict on damages. Each side was instructed to pay their own legal costs and Newton Heath were awarded damages of a solitary farthing. Perhaps the directors had thought this libel case was a way to pay off some of the club debts. Ultimately, it ended up costing money they could ill afford to misspend.

For Newton Heath the victory in the court case in 1893/94 was one of the few they achieved that season and they again finished bottom of the First Division. Another end-of-season Test match was their dubious reward. Against a confident Liverpool side that had won the Second Division title by eight clear points, Newton Heath went down to a 2–0 defeat. They never played in the top division again. They made an enthusiastic attempt to win promotion, in their new colours of green shirts with gold trim, during their first season in the Second Division. That same season, Newton Heath's long-suffering fans acclaimed what they thought was a new club scoring record when Walsall Town Swifts were sent back to the Midlands after a 14–0 drubbing. They also hailed new signing Joe Cassidy who, on his league debut, scored four goals on what the newspapers described as a "fearfully heavy" pitch. After the Swifts appealed to the Football League over the state of the Bank Street pitch, a replay was ordered. They needn't have bothered because Newton Heath again ran out convincing winners. This time it was 9–0 with Cassidy scoring two.

Players came and went throughout the 1890s but the club remained a Second Division team. Second place was achieved in 1896/97 in the new colours of white shirts and blue shorts (or knickers, as they were known at the time). Again the Test matches proved to be Newton Heath's undoing.

A first victory in the Lancashire Cup with a 2–1 win over Blackburn Rovers was almost the only cheerful event at the cash-strapped club as the end of the century drew nearer. The sale of key players to local rivals and rich Southern League clubs was a symptom of their financial problems. Any profits from a consistent promotion challenge or a good Cup run merely served to reduce the existing debt problems. The opening of a social centre in a disused schoolroom in the Institute at Miles Platting was an interesting attempt to provide facilities for supporters on non-match days and some income for the club. Despite the attraction of a billiards table, it ran at a loss. Inevitably, the centre closed, hastened by the loss (or theft) of all the billiard cues and a bailiff's raid in an attempt to settle some of the outstanding debts.

At the turn of the century, Newton Heath were even deeper in financial trouble. Alf Albut had resigned as secretary, his place being taken by James West who joined from Lincoln. In February 1901, a fund-raising bazaar was held in the St James's Hall in the city centre. The intention was to raise over £1,000 to

In this photograph from 1901, club captain Harry Stafford can be seen in the back row, second from the left.

secure the club's finances and boost it back to the First Division. Good publicity and support was forthcoming from local rivals Manchester City, but the bazaar was not a financial success, and barely covered its costs.

By February 1902, Newton Heath were £2,670 in debt and in danger of following Accrington, Bootle and Darwen out of the league. The future looked bleak.

A meeting of shareholders at New Islington Hall on 18 March 1902 was crucial. Newton Heath needed financial backing. When team captain Harry Stafford stood up to reveal that this was now available, the audience were astonished. Stafford and four businessmen would each invest £200 in the club to help pay off the debts. But how had he found benefactors in the club's hour of need?

For the answer we have to go back to the bazaar held at the St James's Hall in 1901. While the event had not been a financial success, it did have one great result. Harry Stafford had brought along his St Bernard dog, Major. Complete with a collection box, the dog roamed around the stalls gathering donations

for the club, but it went missing. A search proved fruitless; there was no sign of the animal or the collection box. Both were eventually found by John Henry Davies, a wealthy brewer. Wanting the dog for his young daughter, Davies set about finding out who owned the stray animal. He eventually met Harry Stafford, and was made aware of the plight of Newton Heath. In return for support for the club from the wealthy brewer and a few of his business colleagues, Stafford allowed Davies to keep the St Bernard for his daughter.

Harry Stafford and the four businessmen – Mr Jones, James Bown, James Taylor and John Henry Davies – took control of Newton Heath Football Club as a condition of investing in the company and the previous board all resigned. It was also thought that a new name would be appropriate, especially since it was now eight years since the club had been based in the Newton Heath area. So, on 28 April 1902, with the blessing of the Football Association, Newton Heath FC became Manchester United FC. A glorious new chapter in the history of the club was about to unfold.

1902
Newton Heath are in danger of closing. £2,670 in debt, they are bailed out by Harry Stafford and a consortium of businessmen.

1902
Harry Stafford, Mr Jones, James Bown, James Taylor and John Henry Davies take control of Newton Heath.

1902
Newton Heath FC change their name to Manchester United FC.

The brilliant Billy Meredith signed for Manchester United following the decline of Manchester City.

CHAPTER TWO

A SHIFT
IN CLUB
FORTUNES

A change of name, a new venue at Old Trafford, plus local rivals Manchester City's fall from grace helped Manchester United become one of the top football clubs of Edwardian times...

Newton Heath officially became Manchester United on 28 April 1902, less than a week after they had played their final match of the season, a 2–0 win against Chesterfield. The new era brought a change of strip to red shirts and white shorts, and these have remained Manchester United's colours to the present day.

The immense wealth of John Henry Davies soon singled him out as the major benefactor of the club. Davies was a self-made man who had worked as estate agent, innkeeper and brewer. A director and later chairman of both Walker & Homfrays Brewery and the Manchester Brewery Company, he built both these companies into great successes. Davies cared little for football until his meeting with Harry Stafford back in 1901. Before then, he had been known for his support of other sports in the Manchester locality such as bowls and cycling, and for his many gifts to charity. Already wealthy, Davies had married into money. His wife Amy was the daughter of Henry Tate, co-founder of the Tate & Lyle sugar-refining empire. Their combined wealth meant that they could buy almost anything they wanted.

Davies set about reorganizing United's administration and finances. He recognized that Newton Heath's financial problems dated back to 1893 and their eviction from North Road. Since then the club had been without a

major benefactor and an injection of hard cash would work wonders, quickly clearing their longstanding debts. Secretary James West had made considerable inroads into the problem of debt, but there was still much to be done. Davies also realized that success on the pitch would draw large crowds to the Bank Street ground, providing much-needed gate money to keep the club afloat.

Team affairs became the responsibility of James West and Harry Stafford who together set about improving on Newton Heath's pitiful 15th place in the Second Division at the end of 1901/02. Under their stewardship, Manchester United played their first Football League match on 6 September 1902, at Gainsborough Trinity's Northolme ground. United returned jubilantly to Bank Street, Clayton, with both points. Charles Richards's goal secured a 1–0 victory. A week later a crowd of over 20,000 packed into Bank Street to see Manchester United's first home league match, a 1–0 victory over Burton United.

Attendances at Bank Street began to rise, averaging 10,823 in 1902/03 compared with 4,411 in the final season as Newton Heath. Rising attendances were matched by greater success on the pitch. After finishing two places from bottom in 1901/02, United stormed up to fifth place, but they were still well off the pace, 13 points from promotion. With the improvement in the club's fortunes, the fans'

April 1902	September 1902	September 1903
The club strip changes to red shirts and white shorts.	Manchester United play their first league game, against Gainsborough Trinity. United win 1–0.	James West resigns as club secretary. A subsequent FA inquiry results in a ban from the game.

level of expectation also increased. From some quarters there was criticism of James West and his abilities, and loud criticism of some of the players he had bought. Davies had given United £3,000 to strengthen the team and some fans expected that this would lead to an immediate return to the First Division.

An horrendous injury list forced the signing of 22 players during the season, and that immediate return was not forthcoming. Fortunately, United were now on a firm financial and administrative footing and were able to cope with this setback.

For James West, the pressure for success became unbearable and on 28 September 1903, he resigned as secretary of Manchester United. He cited the poor performances of some of the players whom he had been instrumental in signing for the club as the reason for his sudden departure just three weeks into the season. Speculation was rife. Had West jumped or had he been pushed? There is no conclusive answer, but in October 1904 West and Harry Stafford were involved in an FA inquiry into financial irregularities at a number of clubs, including both of those in Manchester. Stafford proclaimed his innocence and declared that everything he had done was purely for the benefit of the club during what had been a very dark hour. Both Stafford and West were found guilty of misconduct and banned from the game until May 1907. In his resignation statement, West declared that he was resigning to avoid embarrassing the board of directors. He may have suspected that the Football Association was beginning to question his activities and resigned before they caught up with him.

Whatever the reason for the departure, there was a silver lining to that particular cloud. On 30 September 1903, Manchester United announced that they had appointed the

John Henry Davies

Burnley secretary James Ernest Mangnall as the new secretary of Manchester United. Joining United on the recommendation of J.J. Bentley, President of the Football League and a Manchester United director, Mangnall became the first Manchester United secretary to wield managerial powers.

Mangnall took over total responsibility for team affairs, including scouting, signing and training the players. His aim was to make United a powerful member of the top division and he used Davies's wealth to that end. In his first season, United were challenging for the runners-up spot until the spring. They eventually finished in third place, a solitary point behind Woolwich Arsenal, the runners-up to champions Preston North End.

Confidence was high during the 1904 close season. The signing of Charlie Roberts from Grimsby on 22 April for a fee of £600 had strengthened United's defence and a strong challenge for promotion was expected. Roberts slotted into a half-back line that would soon be famous across the country. Dick Duckworth, Charlie Roberts and Alec Bell formed one of the most secure defensive lines in the Football League, ably supported by their full-backs Robert Bonthron and Vince Hayes.

United began to gain a reputation for solid defending and for being difficult to beat. In fact, they remained unbeaten from 24 September 1904 until 21 January 1905. Despite this, they still failed in their bid to return to the First Division. A second consecutive third place was their prize at the end of season. They finished three points behind runners-up Bolton Wanderers, having won five more points than they had the previous season.

Pressure was beginning to mount on Mangnall. He had spent considerable sums of Davies's money yet the club was still stuck in the Second Division.

It seemed as though it would be third time

September 1903
James Ernest Mangnall becomes the new secretary of Manchester United, and the first to have managerial powers.

May 1904
United finish the season in third place, behind runners-up Woolwich Arsenal and champions Preston North End.

May 1905
Despite gaining five more points than the previous season, United again finish third spot in Division Two.

lucky at the start of the 1905/06 season. Bristol City were early visitors to Bank Street and some 15,000 spectators saw United demolish the West Country side 5–1. This was Charlie Roberts's first league match as captain of the team, a position he held until 1913.

United had a fantastic season and, ironically, only the outstanding play of Bristol City deprived them of the Second Division championship. A 1–1 draw with third-placed Chelsea before a 60,000 Easter crowd virtually assured United of second place, although it took a victory over Leeds City with three matches remaining to confirm their promotion. Bristol City and United were head and shoulders above the other teams in the division, United finishing a massive nine points ahead of Chelsea. A 6–0 home victory over a totally outclassed Burton United team finished off the season.

Now the challenge was to make an impact in the top division. The omens looked good. In the 1906 FA Cup, United had reached the quarter-finals for the first time since 1897,

defeating Staple Hill and Norwich City before an amazing 5–1 victory over the Cup holders, Aston Villa, in front of a crowd of 35,000 at Bank Street. Only a 2–3 home defeat by Woolwich Arsenal ended United's best Cup run yet.

Meanwhile, across at Hyde Road, Manchester City were a club in turmoil. Still under investigation by the Football Association over illegal payments to players (at a time of restricted wages) and further player transfer irregularities, in August 1905 their star player, Billy Meredith, was suspended for alleged match-fixing. He was transfer-listed in May 1906. Soon afterwards, the FA imposed bans on the directors and the club secretary, while many of the first team were suspended from playing until 1 January 1907. Clubs from all over the country were delighted and were soon eyeing up the City players as potential recruits to their sides once their suspensions had lapsed. The club organized an auction at the Queen's Hotel and the secretaries of other Football League and Southern League clubs

May 1906
Following an excellent season, United finish in second spot, gaining promotion to Division One.

May 1906
Manchester City are in disarray after an investigation that leaves many of their first-team stars suspended.

January 1907
Ernest Mangnall quickly negotiates transfers to United for four of City's suspended stars.

arrived to bid for the City stars – players who only two years before had won the FA Cup.

They were too late. Ernest Mangnall had got there first, quickly negotiating a free transfer for Billy Meredith and soon after that acquiring Sandy Turnbull, Herbert Burgess and Jimmy Bannister. The other clubs were furious that Mangnall had arranged this without their knowledge.

United brought all their new players into action the moment their suspensions expired. On New Year's Day 1907, all four of the former City stars made their debuts in a 1–0 victory over Aston Villa at Bank Street in front of 40,000 spectators. For Sandy Turnbull it was an especially good feeling to be playing again – it was his goal, from a Meredith cross, that won the match. United, renowned for a strong defence, now had a first-rate attacking line and they stormed up the table to finish in eighth place.

After one season in the top division, United were ready for a championship challenge. Three straight wins at the start of 1907/08 showed United's intent and, after a defeat against Middlesbrough, the United bandwagon rolled on with 10 more consecutive wins and an impressive 37 goals.

The team was in irresistible championship-winning form, playing an attractive, controlled passing game. Occasional defeats were brushed aside as they dominated the league campaign. Winning 23 of their 38 league matches, United finished the season with 52 points, nine points ahead of runners-up Aston Villa. Sandy Turnbull had been in fantastic form, especially in the first half of the season. His 25 goals in 30 appearances were a club record, and was one that stood until Jack Rowley hit 26 goals in 1946/47. Manchester United were First Division champions just six years after the liquidation of Newton Heath; for John Davies, the taste of success must have been especially sweet.

To celebrate winning the championship, Davies invited the playing staff back to his home, Moseley Hall in Cheadle, for a celebratory dinner, but first United went to play in Europe. The tour was to the Austro-Hungarian empire and the team played matches in Prague, Vienna and Budapest. Generally welcomed, a match against the Budapest league leaders, Ferencvaros, showed the dark underside of touring abroad. United were unbeaten on tour and had sleepwalked through their games. It was soon noticeable that the Ferencvaros side were no match for United's strong defending and quick, agile forwards. A 7–0 victory, with even goalkeeper Harry Moger getting on the scoresheet, was overshadowed by crowd trouble. The players were attacked on leaving the field and later the rioters made further attacks as they left the ground in carriages.

The *Manchester Evening News* correspondent reported: 'Many arrests were made and the police were compelled to draw their swords.'

It was an unhappy end to what had generally been a successful tour. Mangnall said that United would never return to Budapest.

Before setting out on their tour, United had been invited to compete in the very first FA Charity Shield match. A 1–1 draw at Stamford Bridge with the champions of the Southern League, Queen's Park Rangers, forced the Football Association to organize a replay. It took place the following season and this time United ran out easy 4–0 victors to become the inaugural winners of the Shield.

In 1908/09, after a seven-match unbeaten start to the season, United's league form deserted them. They did manage to complete a league double over Manchester City, but this was scant consolation as the club plummeted down the table. A 13th-place finish was a huge disappointment, but they did find form in the FA Cup.

Narrow wins over Brighton and Everton were followed by a 6–1 demolition of Blackburn Rovers in the third round. The quarter-finals brought them up against Ernest Mangnall's old club, Burnley. In the middle of a dismal league run, United seemed to be heading out of the Cup as well. Burnley took

TIMELINE

May 1907
Bolstered by their new signings, United climb up the table to finish eighth.

May 1908
Manchester United are crowned First Division champions.

May 1908
United play in the first Charity Shield, a 1–1 draw with Queen's Park Rangers. In the replay, United run out 4–0 winners.

the lead and held on as the weather conditions deteriorated. A snowstorm descended from the Pennines and, as the pitch became even more of a quagmire and as the markings became obliterated, the referee abandoned the match. Famously, he was so cold and exhausted he was unable to blow his whistle, passing it to Charlie Roberts to call an end to the proceedings.

There were only 18 minutes left on the clock and from then on, perhaps United's name was on the Cup. The match was replayed four days later and the team at last hit some form and left Turf Moor with both a 3–2 victory and a semi-final place. Then came the stiffest test yet – Newcastle United. While Manchester United's league form had been faltering, Newcastle appeared to be en route to becoming the first double-winning team of the twentieth century. Harold Halse spoiled their party by scoring the only goal of the game.

For the first time in their history, Manchester United had reached the final. The FA Cup was regarded as the country's premier competition.

Bristol City were United's opponents and for some of the fans, and especially some of the newspaper correspondents, the match was a straight battle between Charlie Roberts and Billy Wedlock. Wedlock was the man preferred by the England selectors and the game was seen as a chance to prove who was the rightful first-choice international.

The teams had played each other twice a few weeks before the final, with Bristol winning 1–0, followed by a 0–0 draw.

As United and Bristol City both normally played in red shirts, they both changed colours. Bristol chose blue while United took to the field wearing white shirts with a red V. These shirts had been purchased from Billy Meredith's sports shop in Manchester and were presented to the players by the music-hall star George Robey.

United kicked off and they started well, quickly putting pressure on the Bristol defence in the first 10 minutes. They carried on in that

Charlie Roberts was one of the first great Manchester United captains.

vein and when Harold Halse fired a shot against the bar from a cross by Meredith, Clay, the Bristol goalkeeper, was powerless. Sandy Turnbull, reacting quickest to the loose ball, put away the rebound. It was 1–0 to United with 22 minutes on the clock. Turnbull had been a major injury doubt before the match and was nursing a heavily bandaged thigh. Team captain Charlie Roberts felt so confident of Turnbull's striking prowess that he declared he wanted Turnbull in the team, despite the injury, as he could still be a match-winner.

Despite the best efforts of both sets of players, the game became very scrappy with few real goalmouth chances. Tempers frayed towards the end and the referee warned United's players for time-wasting. Vince Hayes went off injured with a broken rib, but United

May 1909
Sandy Turnbull scores the winner as United beat Bristol City 1–0 to win their first FA Cup final.

July 1909
Footballers are ordered by the FA to resign from the Players' Union. United players refuse.

July 1909
United players are forced to train at the Manchester Athletic Club, where the famous 'Outcasts' photo is taken.

reorganized and the 10 men managed to hold on to claim a first FA Cup final victory.

For the large number of Mancunians in the crowd, it was time to celebrate. Charlie Roberts walked up the steps to receive the FA Cup from Lord Charles Beresford. Then it was on to a dinner at the Crystal Palace followed by a night out at the Alhambra music hall.

United's return to Manchester brought huge crowds on to the streets:

The London train hove into sight, and amid a scene of wild enthusiasm Mr Mangnall emerged carrying the Cup on high, followed by the players, their wives, and other people who had travelled from the Metropolis. The band struck up "See the Conquering Hero Comes" and there was a great scramble by the crowd, which had been permitted to enter the platform, to reach the players. Some were carried shoulder high, and ultimately were comfortably seated in the third waggonette. Sticks were waved and hats were thrown in the air and the enthusiasm was unbounded when Roberts, carrying the trophy, came into view.

Manchester Evening News, 27 April 1909

With the FA Cup sitting in the Bank Street trophy cabinet, John Davies's bankrolling of Ernest Mangnall's player purchases was vindicated, although the Football Association soon had something to say about the way the club was being run.

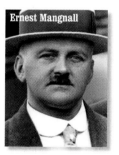
Ernest Mangnall

Although United was registered as a limited company, and had been since 1907, the FA condemned the club as a private monopoly of John Davies that seldom published accounts and was extravagantly managed. An investigation was organized (possibly in a fit of pique after they discovered that United had had a replica of the FA Cup made and presented it to Mr Davies). Reporting in 1910, the FA Committee recommended that United be '…properly constituted and managed in accordance with the requirements of the Football Association'.

They also recommended that United issue shares to the general public and make arrangements for much tighter accounting procedures.

During the 1909 close season, United's players become involved in the battle for players' rights. The Players' Union had been set up in 1898, but by 1908 it was a spent force. However, under the influence of Billy Meredith and Charlie Roberts, it found a new lease of life. This provoked a strong reaction from the Football League who, after the union affiliated itself to the Federation of Trades Unions, tried to destroy it. Players were ordered to resign from the union or be suspended by the FA, but United's players stood by the union. On 1 July they were suspended, which shocked the football world. The FA Cup-winning players were banned from Bank Street and forced to train at the Manchester Athletic Club ground in Fallowfield. It was here that the famous 'Outcasts' photograph was taken, gaining the players more publicity and support.

It was a desperate time for them. Locked out of Bank Street, they were unable to claim their summer wages. Annoyed at their treatment, Sandy Turnbull and a few other players marched into the Bank Street ground and removed some items that were soon to be found on sale in a local pub. Charlie Roberts had them swiftly returned to the club.

Roberts was a prime target for the football authorities. By enticing his resignation from the union, the FA hoped that he would bring the other players with him. Roberts, however, was made of sterner stuff. He, and the other United players, could have resigned from the Players' Union in July and rejoined in September, once the football season had started. But for Roberts a principle was at stake and despite being due a substantial benefit that season, he and the rest of the players stood firm.

TIMELINE

August 1909
An FA committee recommends that United be managed in line with other clubs, with tighter accounting procedures.

September 1909
All 27 of United's players are suspended until a last-minute backdown from the FA, who finally recognise the union.

May 1910
United finish the league season in fifth place.

Manchester United's 1910/11 league championship-winning team line up at their new Old Trafford stadium.

United tried to postpone their first league match of the season – all 27 of their players were suspended. Eventually a truce was called and the league programme started, but despite a full settlement being agreed in October 1909, the FA found it difficult to stop United's players from openly supporting the union.

Never consistent enough to mount a challenge for the title, United finished in fifth place. The real story of the season was United's move away from the noxious fumes and poor playing surface at Bank Street to a brand new, spacious and costly stadium on the other side of Manchester. It is now one of the most famous stadiums in football – Old Trafford.

United started the 1910/11 season in phenomenal form, winning seven of their first eight matches and going on to win the title.

The following season, 1911/12, United barely got into gear. There were terrible problems with injuries and illness all season, and it took two wins in the last three matches to drag the club to safety. For long-serving secretary-manager Ernest Mangnall, this was his last season in charge of the club.

United's great side was breaking up, and over the next few years the club became one of the also-rans in the First Division. Supporters, increasingly affected by wartime regulations, stayed away. Then news leaked out that United's players had been involved in a match-fixing scandal. Following an inquiry, eight players were banned for life – United's Enoch West, Arthur Whalley and Sandy Turnbull, four Liverpool players and a Chester player. The deception was purely about money. As a result of the escalating hostilities, the players realized that organized league football was coming to an end and they saw this as a last chance to make some money before the war ruined their careers or even cost them their lives.

Many players found that their careers were cut short by the war and they were too old to resume playing when peace eventually broke out in 1918. Others, including Sandy Turnbull, the disgraced goalscorer in United's 1909 FA Cup victory, were killed in action.

June 1910
United move from Bank Street to their new, and permanent stadium – Old Trafford.

May 1911
After some superb performances, United end the season as league champions.

May 1912
In his last season in charge of the club, Ernest Mangnall struggles to overcome numerous injuries to players and United just avoid relegation.

Up in the air: the period between the wars proved to be a frustrating period for Manchester United.

CHAPTER THREE

THE IN-BETWEEN YEARS

Between the wars, Manchester United endured their least successful era. There were no league championships or FA Cup victories to celebrate and at one point Third Division football beckoned...

The years between the two world wars contributed virtually nothing to Manchester United's emergence as one of the illustrious names in the world of sport. Of all the various eras that comprise the club's remarkable history, this one is without doubt the least auspicious. Not one single top honour found its way to Old Trafford in the 20 seasons that linked the two conflicts.

It isn't just the lack of success that sets this largely depressing spell apart from the rest; it is also the damaging lack of consistency. In a continual switchback ride, the club lurched back and forth between the top two divisions and almost made an unprecedented fall into the third grade. United succeeded in finishing above halfway in the First Division table just once, in the 1925/26 season. The rest of the time was spent languishing in the lower reaches, or in the Second Division.

If United's performances in the league championship left a great deal to be desired, there was little to console their long-suffering fans when it came to the FA Cup. Twenty appearances in the competition ended in almost blanket disappointment – a lone run to the semi-final in 1926 and another to the sixth round two years later provided the only relief in what must have felt like endless barren years.

At the onset of the First World War, United supporters could have been excused for hoping that the enforced break from fully organized football would help their team to resolve some of the ailments from the immediately preceding years. The glory years of the Roberts-Meredith-Turnbull era had given way to a poor sequence of seasons, which culminated in an 18th-place finish in 1914/15, the last full season before war interrupted regular league football. United, with 30 points from 38 games finished just two places and a couple of points above Tottenham Hotspur, who were relegated and destined to resume, following the cessation of hostilities, in the Second Division.

United therefore approached the return to serious competition without any immediate past glories to emulate. Several players, most notably Billy Meredith, Arthur Whalley (who was severely wounded in Belgium – and had his life ban rescinded), Wilf Woodcock and Jackie Mew, bridged the four inactive football years and reclaimed their places when the players reconvened to ready themselves for 1919/20. One illustrious name from the pre-war days was missing – Sandy Turnbull, one of the great stars of United's first successful side that won the league championship in 1908 and 1911, and in between lifted the FA Cup, lost his life on active service in France in 1917. Turnbull carved his own indelible mark on United history by scoring the only goal in the 1909 Cup final against Bristol City.

TIMELINE

May 1915
In the last full season before war in Europe interrupted regular league football, United narrowly avoid relegation.

May 1920
A mediocre 1919/20 season ends with United in 12th place.

May 1921
At the end of the season, Billy Meredith leaves to join Manchester City. He had played more than 300 games for United.

The United team line up in 1919/20.

John Robson, who had become manager in 1914, retained his position in charge of team affairs. The first side he selected contained several players who were to become the nucleus of United teams for years to come. His teamsheet for the opening Football League Division Two game of the season, against Derby County at the Baseball Ground, included goalkeeper Jackie Mew, full-backs Charlie Moore and Jack Silcock, and centre-half Clarence "Lal" Hilditch. All four – Moore, Silcock and Hilditch were making their debuts – were destined for lengthy and distinguished Old Trafford careers. They were joined by another young man who was set fair for a remarkable career – Joe Spence, a north-easterner from Northumberland. He pulled on the No. 9 shirt for that opening-day match against the Rams, but would later gain fame for his mercurial wing play.

Wilf Woodcock scored and United gained a point from the 1–1 draw against Derby, the team that had finished the 1914/15 season as Second Division champions.

The season began slowly for United and continued that way, stop-starting between average and poor. It never looked like providing anything more than a mid-table finish and United eventually ended in 12th place.

If the first season back had provided little in the way of optimism for United's loyal supporters, the following term was hardly any better. The make-up of the team was much the same as the previous season and the success ratio showed only a minute improvement. They completed the season with 40 points, precisely the same number as the previous season, but they were compiled with two extra victories.

At the end of the season, Billy Meredith left. He was the original Welsh Wizard and one of the greatest players ever to wear the famous red shirt. The spindly-legged genius had been

TIMELINE

September 1921
United are trounced 5–0 by Everton in their first match of the season.

October 1921
John Robson resigns as manager. His replacement is John Chapman, former boss of Airdrieonians.

May 1922
United are relegated to Division Two, after finishing bottom of the table.

with United since 1906, playing in more than 300 league and Cup games for the club. He was instrumental in the successes of 1908 and 1911 when the league title was won, and in the FA Cup triumph of 1909. A quite remarkable man, and natural athlete, he was far from finished and later that summer signed for Manchester City where he continued to display wonderful skills for a further three years.

The 1921/22 season dawned with a catastrophic 5–0 defeat against Everton at Goodison Park, which provided a gloomy but ultimately accurate omen for the forthcoming campaign. If the previous couple of seasons had given United supporters little to get excited about, this one was going to be decidedly bereft of favourable results and enjoyable moments.

United lost their next match 3–2 at home to West Bromwich Albion, but gained some revenge for the opening-day mauling on Merseyside by defeating Everton 2–1 at Old Trafford. The win briefly blew away the black clouds from Old Trafford, but in the next few weeks they returned to the skies above Warwick Road. Five draws and a defeat in the next six games led to United taking up a lowly place in the First Division table. The unfavourable results also led to John Robson resigning his position as manager to be replaced by former Airdrie boss John Chapman.

The spectre of relegation loomed large for most of the season and everyone's worst fears were realized when the

Walter Crickmer

season reached its finale with United four points adrift of Bradford City, who were also relegated, and eight points behind Everton, who managed to avoid the trapdoor.

It was the first time United had suffered the drop since their Newton Heath days back in 1893/94, but the new season opened brightly, bolstered by the signing of Frank Barson, a former Barnsley and Aston Villa star and one of most uncompromising defenders of his day.

If the acquisition of Barson was designed to stiffen the Reds' defence, as the season unfolded it became clear that the decision to recruit him had been a shrewd piece of thinking. United didn't take the Second Division by storm, but they enjoyed a steady season, finishing in fourth place with 48 points, five behind Notts County, the champions. They lost just 11 games all season – one fewer than County – but failed to accumulate sufficient points because they won 17 games and drew 14 compared with the Meadow Lane club's 23 wins and seven draws.

The 1923/24 season began in encouraging style with United winning their first three fixtures. Bristol City were beaten 2–1 at Ashton Gate on the opening day of the season, and back at Old Trafford the Reds defeated Southampton 1–0, and then completed a rapid league double over Bristol City with a 2–1 win.

This early flourish was soon nipped in the bud with none of the following six games ending on a winning note. The last of this less-than-ideal sequence provided one of the rarest statistics in football history when United met Oldham Athletic at Boundary Park on Saturday 6 October 1923. Oldham defender Sam Wynne scored four goals that day, but it didn't help his side to an emphatic win over the near-neighbours. The trouble was that he bagged two goals for his own side – one of them from the penalty spot – and a couple for United. Fortunately for Wynne, his team-mate Billy Howson found the net to give the Latics a 3–2 win. United got a measure of revenge the following weekend when the teams faced each other at Old Trafford with Jimmy Bain scoring twice in a 2–0 victory.

However, fewer games were won than were lost, and United finished the season in 14th position, two points behind local rivals Stockport County.

May 1923
United's first season in Division Two since 1893/94 ends with them finishing in fourth place.

May 1924
After a promising start, United fade into mid-table mediocrity to end the season in 14th place.

May 1925
United find some form – going on a blistering run of seven consecutive wins. They maintain their momentum to earn promotion back to the top flight.

MANCHESTER UNITED **OFFICIAL MEMBERS' HISTORY BOOK**   **25**

Lancelot Holliday Richardson, United goalkeeper, 1925-1929

win against Leicester City, the only side who were to finish higher in the table. This was a satisfactory start, but then the team went on the road to play Stockport County and Stoke City with a return of just one point. They lost 2–1 to County at Edgeley Park and played out a goalless draw with the Potters. It seemed that United, despite that encouraging start, were set for another dismal winter. But then the team assembled a blistering seven-match winning run which registered them among the serious promotion candidates.

It was easily the best sequence of the season, and it was sufficient to launch United on the road back to the First Division. They ended the season just two points behind champions Leicester, who amassed 59 points. United's defence proved to be their strongest department, conceding only 23 goals, the least by any team in the division.

Among the players who ended the season in United's first team was centre-forward Albert Pape, who had joined the club in rather unusual circumstances the previous February. Pape, who had played for Rotherham County and Notts County earlier in his career, was in Manchester with his Clapton Orient teammates making ready for a league fixture at Old Trafford. With the kick-off less than two hours away, a deal was struck and he was transferred to United. He took his place in the side and they beat Clapton 4–2. To crown a remarkable day, Pape scored one of United's goals. His stay at Old Trafford lasted barely nine months before he returned south to play for Fulham.

After three seasons in the Second Division, a return to the top grade came as a breath of fresh air to club and fans alike. John Chapman was still in charge and pinned his faith on the squad that had taken United up a few months before.

The first season after promotion is always looked upon as one of consolidation and that's just what United achieved during 1925/26. They didn't get carried away with ambitious thoughts of the championship, but they did accumulate 44 points, enough to finish a

After four seasons of largely uninspiring fare, United's success-starved supporters were given something to cheer when in 1924/25 the team won promotion back to the top grade. During the 42-match programme, they lost just eight times, and only one of those defeats, against Oldham Athletic, came at Old Trafford.

United began the season with a 1–0 home

TIMELINE

January 1926
City inflict an appalling 6–1 defeat on United in the Manchester derby at Old Trafford.

April 1926
Old Trafford plays host to its first full international – a 1–0 victory for Scotland against England.

May 1926
Local rivals Manchester City are relegated to the Second Division.

26   MANCHESTER UNITED **OFFICIAL MEMBERS' HISTORY BOOK**

highly creditable ninth in the table, 13 points behind Huddersfield Town, who became the first club to win the league championship for a third consecutive year. The high point of the league programme came in late April when Sunderland, who finished third in the table, were beaten 5–1 at Old Trafford. The lowest moment was a 6–1 mauling by City in the Manchester derby at Old Trafford.

Old Trafford, one of the most capacious and well appointed club grounds in the country, was finally honoured with its first full international on 17 April 1926 when Scotland beat England 1–0, Alex Jackson scoring the goal in front of 49,000 fans.

With City having departed to the Second Division, it was left to United to carry the flag for Manchester, but there was little to celebrate as the 1926/27 season unfolded. Inconsistency was the main feature of the campaign with the Reds taking both points from just 13 of their 42 league fixtures. The team once again relied heavily on the scoring instincts of Joe Spence who bagged 18 goals. Two changes at managerial level did little to promote stability. John Chapman remained in charge until October and was then replaced by Clarence Hilditch who became player-manager before handing over the reins to Herbert Bamlett the following April.

Despite the occasional upheavals, the season ended with United in a comfortable 15th position. Any hopes of making a name for themselves in the FA Cup evaporated when they were knocked out in the third round by Second Division Reading after two replays.

Herbert Bamlett's first full season at the helm brought little respite from the mediocrity that had haunted the club since the end of the First World War. United won three more games than they had the previous season and amassed just one point fewer, but it didn't prevent them from slipping to 18th spot in the First Division table. United avoided relegation by a single point, but there was some consolation to be had in the FA Cup. Brentford were hammered 7–1 at Old Trafford in the

third round as United set off on another encouraging Cup run. Bury were beaten, after a replay, in the next round, and Birmingham City came a cropper at Old Trafford in the last 16. Sadly, the Reds' luck ran out in the sixth round when Blackburn Rovers, who eventually lifted the trophy, beat them 2–0 at Ewood Park.

United did, however, finish the league campaign on a high note by trouncing Liverpool 6–1 at Old Trafford, with Joe Spence, almost inevitably, grabbing a hat-trick.

The 1928/29 season threatened to be one of ultimate disappointment. United won just four of 27 fixtures from the opening day, but a remarkable recovery staged during the last third of the term, which included a spell of seven wins in nine games, averted a plunge into the second grade and hoisted the club into a respectable 12th place in the table.

On the Cup front, it was another short-lived interest with the Reds knocking out Port Vale before being eliminated themselves by neighbours Bury.

"Here we go again" must have been the phrase on United supporters' lips just three days into the 1929/30 season after the Reds had lost the opening couple of fixtures, to Newcastle United and Leicester City, both 4–1 and both away. The rot was halted briefly with a mini-revival of three straight victories, but that renewed hope gave way to further despair as the next six games all ended in defeat. That run of unfavourable results amounted to the worst sequence of the season, but there was still very little to cheer the faithful in the months that followed as United finished below halfway yet again. Defeat at the hands of Swindon Town of the Third Division (South) in the FA Cup helped to keep the club in the doldrums.

United's struggle to retain their place among the country's elite had become increasingly more difficult, but each year they always pulled something out of the bag to preserve their First Division status. That was until the first complete season of the Thirties when United's

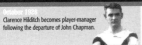

October 1926
Clarence Hilditch becomes player-manager following the departure of John Chapman.

April 1927
Herbert Bamlett takes over as manager of Manchester United.

January 1928
Despite going to two replays, United cannot overcome Second Division Reading and exit the FA Cup at the third round stage.

MANCHESTER UNITED **OFFICIAL MEMBERS' HISTORY BOOK**   **27**

reserves of luck and resolve finally ran dry. Twelve consecutive defeats from the start of the season virtually sealed United's fate as they became racing certainties for the drop. Two home wins, 2–0 against Birmingham City and 2–1 versus Derby County, were all the fans were given to cheer in the first half of the campaign. It was only marginally better after Christmas as the club slid towards the bottom of the table.

United eventually completed the season with a pitiful seven wins to their name – the worst return since the early 1890s. Needless to say, they finished bottom, nine points adrift of Leeds United who were also relegated. Amazingly, they managed to beat Sheffield Wednesday, league champions in the previous two seasons, 4–1, but it was a rare bright moment amid the almost constant gloom. Manager Bamlett became a victim of the club's failure and his duties were taken over by secretary Walter Crickmer.

United's involvement in the FA Cup ended in the fourth round with a 1–0 defeat at Grimsby Town. That came after a protracted third-round tie with Stoke City that stretched to a second replay at Anfield, which United won 4–2.

The following couple of seasons produced little to generate any real optimism with modest finishes in the Second Division and early exits from the FA Cup, but at least it went a good way to preparing club and supporters alike for the real scare that lay ahead at the climax of the 1933/34 season.

The club had good reason to thank local businessman James Gibson for his benevolence late in 1931 when he agreed to a cash injection to ease financial problems. He later became club chairman. Second Division Plymouth Argyle dumped United out of the Cup in 1932 while the Reds were shown the door by Middlesbrough 12 months later. United were now managed by Scott Duncan, who had taken the helm before the start of the 1932/33 campaign.

There was an emotional departure for the great Joe Spence during the 1933 close season when he left after a fabulous 14 years at Old Trafford. He moved on to play for Bradford City and later, Chesterfield. Joe was the first player to appear in more than 500 games – 510 to be precise – and he scored a total of 168 league and Cup goals.

United got the 1933/34 season off on the wrong foot with a 4–0 defeat against Plymouth Argyle at Home Park and rarely showed much sign of improvement as the winter months progressed. They suffered several heavy defeats – 5–1 at home to Bolton Wanderers, 6–1 at Bradford Park Avenue, 5–1 at Lincoln City and 7–3 at Grimsby Town – as they became engrossed in the relegation dogfight.

These poor results coupled with numerous other less spectacular defeats left United staring at the very real prospect of dropping into the Third Division for the first time. They were in 21st position in the table with 32 points when they travelled to the Den to play Millwall in the final match of the season. The Lions, in 20th place with 33 points, needed just

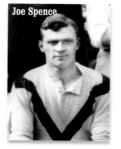

Joe Spence

a draw to escape relegation and send United tumbling. It was a close call but ultimately United came through the challenge. Goals from John Cape and Tommy Manley gave them an enormously important 2–0 win. Without question, in playing terms, it was the lowest point in the club's history and from then on the only way was up.

Nevertheless, the remaining five seasons before the dark clouds of war began to gather over Europe once more were spent commuting between the top two divisions. At least there was enough happening on a regular basis to keep the fans' attention.

TIMELINE

January 1928
Manchester United trounce Brentford 7–1 in the third round of the FA Cup.

March 1928
United's Cup run comes to an end in the sixth round, where they are beaten 2–0 by Blackburn Rovers, who go on to win the trophy.

May 1928
Relegation is avoided by a single point but the season ends on something of a high with a 6–1 mauling of Liverpool in the final match of the campaign.

United finished fifth in the Second Division 12 months after their close shave at Millwall. George Mutch was leading scorer with 18 goals as the Reds finished 11 points behind Brentford, the champions.

The improvement gave a foretaste of what was in store for the following season when United proceeded to win their first title, albeit that of the Second Division, since 1911. The Reds lost just eight games throughout the campaign, one less than Charlton Athletic, who finished runners-up. Mutch was again instrumental in United's success with 21 goals. Harry Rowley wasn't far behind with 19 to his credit.

Happiness quickly turned to despair once again, when after just one term in the top grade United found themselves heading back to the Second Division at the end of the 1936/37 campaign. Another poor season concluded with just 10 wins on the board and United were consigned to the drop along with Sheffield Wednesday. It was their last relegation for almost 40 years. In the FA Cup, United defeated Reading in the third round for the second successive year before suffering a 5–0 drubbing at Arsenal.

Included in United's defence for most of the latter part of the season was Oldham-born half-back Walter Winterbottom, who was to become England manager after the war.

The club's yo-yo existence continued. They moved in an upwardly mobile direction at the close of the 1937/38 season, claiming the runners-up spot and a return to a place among football's elite. Johnny Carey, Stanley Pearson and Jack Rowley, three players who were to make their mark in the great United side of the early post-Second World War era, all made their debut during the season.

Cup glory, however, still eluded them. Brentford knocked them off the road to Wembley in the fifth round.

The return to the top grade proved to be an uneventful season apart from avoiding a swift fall back to the Second Division, which had been their fate two years before. They finished

Stan Pearson, one of the hundreds of players who had their playing careers bisected by the Second World War.

14th in the league and went out of the Cup in the third round to West Bromwich Albion in what was to be the last completed season before the outbreak of war.

Old Trafford's record attendance figure was set on 25 March 1939, but United weren't involved. The match was an FA Cup semi-final between Wolverhampton Wanderers and Grimsby Town – 76,962 fans crammed into Old Trafford and watched Wolves book their place in the final with a 5–1 win.

Just three games were completed at the onset of the 1939/40 season before the programme was halted following the declaration of war. It was to be seven years before the next peacetime league season commenced.

May 1931
An appalling season (only seven wins) ends with United relgated to Division Two.

May 1934
United play Millwall in the final game of the season needing a win to avoid relegation to the Third Division. A vital 2–0 victory keeps the club up.

September 1939
Back in the top flight, United's (and everyone else's) season comes to a premature end with the outbreak of war.

Johnny Carey is lifted up
as United celebrate their
1948 FA Cup win.

CHAPTER FOUR

BUSBY SETS THE STANDARD

The arrival of Matt Busby was to transform Manchester United. His appointment not only reaped league and cup triumphs, it provided the benchmark for future generations...

Manchester City, United's fierce rivals from across town, were the area's premier club during the Twenties and Thirties. League champions and runners-up during those years, City also reached three FA Cup finals, winning the famous trophy in 1934 with a side that included many of the top names of the day.

United fans could be excused for casting envious eyes at their more successful neighbours from Moss Side; and as it turned out, one of the players who helped to bring the FA Cup back to Manchester later moved to Old Trafford to begin the process of transforming them into the most famous club on the planet.

Matt Busby, a Scotsman from Bellshill, Lanarkshire, shared the half-back duties with Sam Cowan and Jackie Bray in that Cup-winning side. He joined City in 1928 and gave the Blues excellent service for eight years as an attacking wing-half, playing in 226 league and Cup games and scoring 14 goals. He also became a full Scottish international when he pulled on the No. 4 shirt against Wales at Ninian Park, Cardiff in October 1933. Wales won 3–2.

Busby's opposite number in that Welsh side was a certain Jimmy Murphy of West Bromwich Albion, who was later to become his trusted friend and lieutenant at Old Trafford. Born in Ton Pentre, South Wales, Murphy spent 11 years at the Hawthorns, during which time he appeared in 223 competitive fixtures for the Baggies – including the 1935 FA Cup final against Sheffield Wednesday – as well as representing his country on 13 occasions.

Matt Busby was just beginning his fifth season with Liverpool when war was declared in September 1939. He had been transferred to Anfield from Manchester City in February 1936. In 1945, with the end of the war in sight, he was offered a job at Liverpool with the backroom staff. Reading, of the Third Division (South), had also approached him to become assistant manager to his good friend Joe Edelston, and Scottish League club Ayr United had offered him employment.

Manchester United, who had been without a manager since Scott Duncan had moved on to Ipswich Town late in 1937, contacted Busby with a view to him taking over the hot seat at Old Trafford.

Busby evaluated all the employment opportunities and after due consultation with his wife Jean, chose United. He accepted the post of manager at Old Trafford on 22 October 1945. Having agreed to take on the task of

October 1945 Manchester United confirm Matt Busby as their new manager. Soon after, Busby appoints Jimmy Murphy as his right-hand man.

October 1945 Busby's first match in charge sees United beat Bolton 2–1. Due to bomb damage, United continue to play their home matches at Maine Road.

May 1947 United finish the season strongly but miss out on the League title by one point to Liverpool.

Busby had a clear vision of how he believed the game should be played.

returning United to their pre-First World War trophy-winning ways, the Red Devils' new boss set about recruiting a right-hand man.

His opportunity arrived late in 1945 when, still in the forces, he was passing through Bari, in Italy. There he bumped into Jimmy Murphy, whom by then he had faced many times on the soccer field. Murphy had been a redoubtable opponent and a player Busby would have preferred to be playing with than against. So on a warm day in southern Italy, having listened to Murphy talking about football to a gathering of army lads, Busby decided that here was the man he wanted to join him at United. Once Murphy had completed his training session, Busby moved in to make his first recruitment as manager of Manchester United. There and then they shook hands on the partnership that was destined to become one of the greatest double acts football would ever see.

The architects of United's rebuilding programme were now in place and Busby was under no illusions about the enormous task that lay ahead. United was a club on its knees with little financial clout, a bomb-damaged ground and a set-up that had well and truly forgotten how to succeed on the field. On the credit side, he had inherited several players who would eventually form the nucleus of United's first great side in almost 40 years.

Busby's first match in charge was a Football War League (North) game against Bolton Wanderers at Maine Road on Saturday 27 October 1945. His first-ever selection lined up as follows: Jack Crompton, Joe Walton, John Roach, Jack Warner, Bert Whalley, Henry Cockburn, Harry Worrall, Johnny Carey, Jack Smith, Jack Rowley and Billy Wrigglesworth. Goals from Carey and Worrall gave them a 2–1 win. Other players who made appearances in that final war season and who proved to be valuable assets in future years included Allenby Chilton, Stan Pearson, John Aston, Charlie Mitten and Jimmy Delaney.

The FA Cup returned to the calendar during the 1945/46 campaign. Just for that season it was decided to play the rounds over two legs.

TIMELINE

November 1947
United produce one of their best performances of the season to trounce Wolverhampton Wanderers 6–2 in the league.

January 1948
It's another high-scoring United performance, this time in the FA Cup, as Aston Villa are defeated 6–4 in the third round.

March 1948
A Stan Pearson hat-trick clinches United's first FA Cup final appearance in 39 years.

32 **MANCHESTER UNITED OFFICIAL MEMBERS' HISTORY BOOK**

United were drawn against Accrington Stanley in the third round, playing away at Peel Park in the first match. They held Stanley to a 2–2 draw in Accrington and completed the job in the return with a 5–1 win. In the fourth round United were pitched in against Preston North End, and after winning the home leg 1–0, they were eliminated after losing 3–1 at Deepdale.

So, with the country slowly getting back to some form of normality after six years under the leaden skies of war, football also resumed normal service with a complete 42-match league programme prepared for the start of the 1946/47 season. United were still unable to play home games at Old Trafford, which remained in a state of disrepair after being damaged by enemy action during the war. They played their war league games at Maine Road, and that arrangement was to continue as serious football got under way again.

United's opening fixture was against Grimsby Town (as it had been at the start of the ill-fated 1939/40 season) at Maine Road. They lined up: Jack Crompton, Johnny Carey, Billy McGlen, Jack Warner, Allenby Chilton, Henry Cockburn, Jimmy Delaney, Stan Pearson, Jimmy Hanlon, Jack Rowley and Charlie Mitten. Warner, Carey and Pearson were the only ones who had played in the side that had defeated the Mariners 4–0 at Old Trafford those seven years before. This time the Red Devils won again, but by 2–1 with Mitten and Rowley scoring the goals.

It was an encouraging start to the season and there was plenty more to raise supporters' spirits as their favourites went on to claim maximum points from the subsequent four matches. Chelsea, Charlton Athletic, Liverpool (the eventual champions, who were beaten 5–0 at Maine Road) and Middlesbrough were all despatched as United recorded their best opening to a First Division season in decades. It was a good omen as they went on to challenge for the league title.

The gathering of points slowed somewhat in the weeks that followed, with United winning just one and drawing four of the next eight fixtures. Sunderland's 3–0 win at Maine Road was the only time United lost at their temporary headquarters. They ended the season just one point behind Liverpool. The teams met at Anfield during the closing weeks of the campaign and a single first-half goal from Albert Stubbins was enough to give Liverpool the points. United finished the season with two home wins against Portsmouth (3–0) and Sheffield United (6–2), but it wasn't enough to snatch the title.

Football was enjoying a post-war boom with interest sky-high and attendances running at enormous levels. United had pleased their fans with a good first season and that vast improvement on what had been served up during the pre-war days was continued the following year.

United opened the 1947/48 First Division fixture programme with a trip to the north east to face Middlesbrough at Ayresome Park. Jack Rowley grabbed both goals in a 2–2 draw as Busby's team got off to a satisfactory start. In those days of two points for a win and one for draw, sharing the spoils while on excursion was looked on as equally acceptable as winning on home territory.

United returned to Maine Road to entertain Liverpool in midweek and Charlton Athletic the following Saturday. Both games provided good victories with the Mersey Reds being beaten 2–0 and the Londoners losing 6–2.

It was an extremely encouraging start to the season, but that three-match, five-point opening was followed by a lamentable sequence of nine games without a win. A 2–0 home win over Aston Villa in late October brought the poor run to an end and the very next Saturday United recorded one of their best wins of the campaign when they slammed Wolverhampton Wanderers 6–2 at Molineux. Surprisingly, Rowley, who finished the season as top scorer with 23 league goals, failed to find the net. The half-dozen goals were shared among his co-attackers – Morris and Pearson netted two each, Delaney and Mitten contributed one each.

May 1948
United finish as runners-up in the league for a second successive season, this time behind champions Arsenal.

May 1948
United come from 2–1 behind to beat Blackpool 4–2 in the 1948 FA Cup final.

August 1948
Pre-season optimism takes a dent as United lose their first game of the season, 2–1 at home to Derby County.

Manchester United line up in 1947.

The FA Cup challenge began in the second week of January with an away tie against Aston Villa – and what a tie it turned out to be! The huge crowd of 58,683 packed into Villa Park was enthralled by an astonishing match that many claim to be one of the greatest ever played in the competition. United eventually won 6–4, but the outcome remained in the balance right up until the final minutes.

United were drawn at home to Liverpool, but with Old Trafford still out of action and Maine Road unavailable (with City having drawn a home tie against Chelsea), the match was switched to Everton's Goodison Park. Another vast crowd, this time numbering 74,721, witnessed a terrific encounter which ended with United 3–0 winners.

The same scenario applied in the following round when both United and City drew home games, so the fifth-round tie against Charlton Athletic went ahead at Leeds Road, the home ground of Huddersfield Town. The Yorkshire air obviously agreed with United, as they reached the last eight, courtesy of a 2–0 win.

In the quarter-final, United were again drawn at home this time against Preston North End, who had ousted Manchester City at Maine Road in the previous round. North End, with great players including Bill Shankly and Tom Finney in their line-up, were one of the country's top sides in those days, but they couldn't repeat their fifth-round success and United ran out 4–1 winners.

Busby had guided United to their first FA Cup semi-final in 22 years and the Red half of Manchester was gripped with Cup fever. Derby County stood between United and their first Wembley final. Hillsborough staged the game and United completed their run to the final, with Stan Pearson scoring a hat-trick in the 3–1 win.

So for the first time in 39 years, United supporters became engaged in the annual scramble for Cup final tickets. Blackpool, boasting the talents of Stanley Matthews and Stanley Mortensen, were the opponents and those fans lucky enough to obtain a precious ticket were treated to a terrific match. United, playing in a change strip of royal blue shirts, twice fell behind. Jack Rowley's 30th-minute goal was sandwiched between Eddie Shimwell's 14th-minute penalty and Mortensen's strike 10 minutes before the interval.

With 20 minutes of the match remaining, the Seasiders looked destined to spoil United's day but three goals – from Rowley, Stan Pearson and Johnny Anderson – clinched a 4–2 comeback win.

It was a great moment for United, for Manchester and for Matt Busby who had restored the club to trophy-winning status in only his second full season. Manchester went wild with jubilation when the gleaming trophy was paraded through the streets of the city and shown to a vast throng waiting in Albert Square. The club's supporters had waited a long time to see their team emerge from the shadows and they were determined to enjoy this momentous event to the full.

United also made a fine showing in the league after that early poor run. Arsenal took the title, but United finished as runners-up for the second successive season. The Red Devils really were back in business.

There were high hopes that it would be third time lucky as the 1948/49 season opened towards the end of August. United started with a home game against Derby County, but the eager anticipation of the huge crowd gathered inside Maine Road was stifled as United went down 2–1. It wasn't the ideal launch to a campaign which many people hoped and believed could bring them the league championship for the first time since before the First World War. Early disillusionment was quickly nipped in the bud when United proceeded to win their next two fixtures. A 3–0 win over Blackpool at Bloomfield Road was followed by an even more impressive triumph as Busby and his team returned from

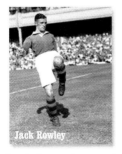
Jack Rowley

Highbury having defeated Arsenal, the reigning champions, 1–0 in front of almost 65,000 fans.

Buoyed by their team's spectacular away wins, United's supporters looked forward to the next match with some relish. It was the return fixture with Blackpool at Maine Road and, having enjoyed a day by the seaside the previous week, an early double over the Tangerines was predicted. Unfortunately, Blackpool were reading from a different script and took their revenge with a 4–3 win.

Unpredictability was to be a feature of the early part of the season as the team sought to find some consistency. Only three of the next nine matches ended with the points in United's possession and it wasn't until the middle segment of the campaign that they finally clicked into serious point-gathering form. During the run-up to Christmas, they put together a sequence of results that included a half-dozen wins and an equal number of draws. As a result of that improved stability, they were installed among the title contenders as the New Year dawned.

On the second weekend of January, United began the journey along the road they hoped would end in a second successive visit to Wembley. Bournemouth and Boscombe Athletic travelled north to provide the opposition in the third round, but were sent tumbling out of the competition after losing 6–0 at Maine Road.

Bradford Park Avenue were next and United eventually overcame them, but it took three matches. The original fourth-round tie, played at Maine Road, ended 1–1 as did the replay at Park Avenue. United finally stepped forward to the fifth round after they had trounced the Yorkshire club 5–0 in the third match back at Moss Side.

That season's fourth round provided one of

May 1949
Yet again, United finish the season in second place, although they do beat the champions, Portsmouth, on the final day of the season.

August 1949
United leave their temporary home of Maine Road and return to a refurbished Old Trafford. Their first match there is a 3–0 victory over Bolton Wanderers.

March 1950
Charlie Mitten scores four, including three from the penalty spot, as United demolish Aston Villa 7–0.

MANCHESTER UNITED **OFFICIAL MEMBERS' HISTORY BOOK** 35

Johnny Carey receives the
FA Cup at Wembley in 1948.

the biggest upsets in the history of the competition. Yeovil Town, of the Southern League, sent shock waves through the country when they defeated First Division Sunderland 2–1 on their famous sloping pitch at The Huish. It was an astonishing win, which sent the green-and-white-shirted heroes forward for a tilt against the Cup holders at Maine Road. An enormous crowd in excess of 81,000 packed the ground for the match. It had all the romance that makes the FA Cup so special.

Most of the country was rooting for underdogs Yeovil, but Busby's team of all-stars won the game 8–0, with Jack Rowley claiming five goals. A 1–0 sixth-round win against Hull City at Boothferry Park moved United into the last four for the second year running, where they came up against Wolverhampton Wanderers. Leicester City and Portsmouth were the other two semi-finalists.

The game was allocated to Sheffield Wednesday's well-appointed headquarters at Hillsborough. Charlie Mitten scored for United; Sammy Smyth netted for Wolves. The tie went to extra-time, but there were no more goals. The 1–1 draw meant that the teams had to meet again, this time on Merseyside at Goodison Park. Another huge crowd gathered and they saw the Black Country club win through to the final with a single goal from Ulsterman Smyth.

Meanwhile, on the league front, United continued to put in a serious challenge for the title, winning seven of their final 10 games. Portsmouth, who lost out to Leicester in the FA Cup semi-final, found huge consolation in winning the league championship. United, for the third successive season, finished in second place. Appropriately, the teams met on the final day of the season at Maine Road. Pompey

April 1950
Jeff Whitefoot's United debut, aged 16 years and 105 days, makes him the youngest player to make a league appearance for the club.

May 1950
United fade towards the end of the league season and finish in fourth place. Portsmouth retain their title.

June 1950
Matt Busby and his side embark on a month-long tour of Canada and the United States.

had already clinched the title, but United, with two goals from Jack Rowley (2) and Charlie Mitten, enjoyed a small slice of compensation with a 3–2 win.

United were proving to be the most consistent side of the early post-war period, but after three good seasons they were still looking for a top-place finish. During the summer of 1949, the club bade farewell to their temporary home at Maine Road and made their long-awaited return to Old Trafford.

United had been forced into exile after Luftwaffe bombs had inflicted severe damage on Old Trafford during air raids in the early 1940s. It wasn't that the German air crews were deliberately trying to demolish the famous football stadium on Warwick Road North. It was just that a few bombs had strayed from the intended target of nearby Trafford Park, at the time one of the biggest industrial estates in the world.

Some matches had been staged at Old Trafford in the early years after the end of the conflict, but the ground wasn't considered ready for the first team until the onset of the 1949/50 season.

Supporters were hoping that a return to their own patch on Warwick Road would prove to be the missing element in converting their team from runners-up to champions. They had done well at Maine Road, losing just seven league matches in three seasons, but there is nowhere like home, so it was with more than the usual feverish excitement that the first home game was anticipated.

The season began with a 1–0 win over Derby County at the Baseball Ground and then it was on to Old Trafford and a meeting with neighbours Bolton Wanderers. The game was played on a Wednesday afternoon, but it still attracted a crowd of more than 40,000, the majority of whom were delighted to see United run out 3–0 winners.

Two matches, two wins was a good start and the encouraging opening continued with United remaining unbeaten in the opening eight games.

By and large, form was maintained and as a result United were installed as one of the front-runners in the championship race. Wolverhampton Wanderers led the field early on with Liverpool taking over the top spot as the season headed towards Christmas. Busby's team were hot on the heels of Liverpool at the turn of the year and it appeared that the title would end up at either Old Trafford or Anfield.

United continued to pick up points on a regular basis and in early March they took over from Liverpool at the head of the table. In one remarkable fixture at Old Trafford, United beat Aston Villa 7–0 with Charlie Mitten scoring four of the goals, three of his haul being claimed from the penalty spot.

United and Liverpool met at Old Trafford in mid-March with Busby's team heading the table by two points. The game ended goalless, leaving United still in pole position with 10 games left to play. Portsmouth, the eventual champions, were trailing United by six points. The Fratton Park club appeared to be one of the outsiders, but by the time they travelled to Old Trafford in mid-April, they had closed to within two points of United who by this time had slipped into second place, a point behind leaders Sunderland.

Pompey, the reigning champions, were not about to give up their title without a fight and goals from Jack Froggatt and Douglas Reid gave them a vital 2–0 win in front of almost 45,000 fans. The match against Portsmouth was a special occasion for Jeff Whitefoot, who was called up to make his league debut at the tender age of 16 years 105 days, which made him the youngest player to make a league appearance for the club. Hopes of landing the championship had begun to evaporate. Portsmouth had made a late charge in defence of their title and in the final outcome they finished top with 53 points, just above Wolves on goal average, one point ahead of Sunderland in third place and three points better off than United in fourth.

At the season's close, United embarked on a month-long tour of the United States and

July 1950
Charlie Mitten leaves United to join Santa Fe FC in Bogota on a lucrative deal that is terminated when Colombia becomes a member of FIFA.

May 1961
United finish the season in second place for the fourth time in five seasons. Tottenham Hotspur are champions.

August 1951
Jack Rowley scores a hat-trick in each of United's first two games of the season.

MANCHESTER UNITED **OFFICIAL MEMBERS' HISTORY BOOK**   **37**

Johnny Carey with his 1949 Footballer of the Year award.

start, losing just three of the first dozen matches. During that spell they remained unbeaten at Old Trafford, a record which did much to ensure that United were once more installed among the contenders for the league championship.

As the season wore on, United stayed, for the best part, in touch with the leaders, but it wasn't until the closing stages that their real credentials began to surface. Tottenham Hotspur had emerged as the frontrunners during the second half of the season and they eventually claimed the title with a four-point advantage over United. Busby's team were forced to settle for second best yet again and there wasn't any consolation where the FA Cup was concerned, United going out in the quarter-finals to Birmingham City at St Andrew's.

The 1951/52 season dawned with many United supporters beginning to wonder if their team was ever going to claim the league championship. They were becoming used to seeing other teams lift the trophy while United were the perennial runners-up. Four times in five seasons they had appeared to be in with an excellent chance of collecting the silverware, but each time they missed out.

The FA Cup triumph in 1948 was a marvellous achievement that everyone cherished and wouldn't have missed for the world. But however happy they were to wallow in the glitz and glamour of the Cup and revel in its unparalleled excitement, the holy grail for them and every other club remained the league title. United had proved beyond all doubt that they were up to the job with a remarkable level of consistency, but they still needed to go that extra mile to claim their first championship in more than 40 years.

The team was packed with top-bracket players – United were one of the top sides of the day and each season opened with optimism brimming over. On Wednesday 22 August 1951, the faithful gathered for the first home game of the season, and this time they were embarking on a voyage that would end

Canada, playing 11 matches in far-flung places including New York, Los Angeles and Toronto.

United began the 1950/51 season with a couple of new faces in their starting line-up. Reg Allen, signed from Queen's Park Rangers, donned the goalkeeper's shirt for the opening game of the campaign, and at No. 4 was Eddie McIlvenny. A few months earlier he had skippered the United States of America side to a famous 1–0 victory over England in a World Cup match in Belo Horizonte, Brazil. McIlvenny retained his place in the side for the next match, but despite staying at Old Trafford for three seasons, he didn't make another competitive appearance. Allen, by contrast, became the club's first-choice keeper for the next couple of seasons. Missing from the line-up was winger Charlie Mitten, who had left to join Colombian club Santa Fe of Bogota.

The club once again got off to a reasonable

TIMELINE

January 1952 United make a surprise early exit in the third round of the FA Cup, going down 2–0 to Second Division Hull City.

May 1952 United win the league after defeating Arsenal 6–1 in the final game of the season. It is United's first championship triumph in 41 years.

June 1952 United again spend the summer on a tour of North America.

38 MANCHESTER UNITED OFFICIAL MEMBERS' HISTORY BOOK

with all their hopes and dreams fulfilled. Middlesbrough provided the opposition that afternoon and they were sent on their way back to Teesside having lost 4–2. Jack Rowley grabbed a hat-trick, his second in four days. He had scored a trio against West Bromwich Albion at the Hawthorns on the season's opening day.

It was a great start for Rowley and an equally satisfactory launch to the campaign for the club. They were, as so often in recent years, instantly looked upon as one of the teams likely to succeed. A series of favourable early results put them at the top of the table on a couple of occasions, but it wasn't all plain sailing. Successive defeats at Tottenham and at home to Preston at the end of September caused them to slip from grace, but overall there were many opportunities to celebrate the collection of two points. As Christmas loomed United found themselves in a good position among the frontrunners.

The basis of the team remained much the same as it had for the previous five seasons, but new players were introduced as the season unfolded. Johnny Berry, an import from Birmingham City, made the right-wing berth his own; Roger Byrne, a future captain, and Jackie Blanchflower both made their debuts in a goalless draw against Liverpool at Anfield.

Any fears that a protracted run in the FA Cup could derail United's championship ambitions were quickly removed when Hull City, of the Second Division, produced a shock 2–0 third-round win at Old Trafford. It was a disappointing early exit, but at least it left the way clear for Busby and his boys to press on with the season's more important work – the task of trying to land the league championship.

Arsenal, Portsmouth and Tottenham Hotspur emerged as the biggest threats to United's ambitions, but as the final day of the season arrived only the Gunners – who, by an amazing quirk of the fixture list, were in Manchester to play United – still had a chance of snatching the title from Busby's grasp. But they would have to beat United by seven clear

goals to take the honour on goal average.

More than 53,000 gathered at Old Trafford to see if United could brush aside Arsenal's challenge and end the long wait for the ultimate in domestic football glory. They had no need to worry. Jack Rowley proceeded to end the season in the same style in which he had opened it by claiming a hat-trick as United stormed to a spectacular 6–1 victory.

The league championship flag was back at Old Trafford for the first time in 41 years and the tag of "champion runners-up" had finally been shed. There was no added prize of European qualification in those days, just the glory of becoming champions of England, but after five seasons of near misses, both United and their supporters were ecstatic.

After another extensive tour of North America, United prepared to defend their title. But it was soon evident that the make-up of the side would need a major overhaul.

The campaign opened poorly with United slipping into the lower reaches of the First Division table after winning just three of the opening 11 fixtures. Concerns were aired in various quarters, but they were alerting Matt Busby to nothing he hadn't already identified.

The team was beginning to age, but he was already making his plans for the future and was quick to declare that there was a deep pool of talent in the club's junior and reserve sides and no cause to worry. His assessment of the situation was to prove uncannily prophetic.

The talented players to whom he referred were youngsters such as Duncan Edwards, David Pegg, Eddie Colman, Wilf McGuinness and Bill Foulkes. Their day was to come.

The first of Busby's great sides was starting to suffer the ravages of time, but they had helped to lay the foundations of a modern Manchester United that would eventually be accepted as one of football's greatest clubs. It was three seasons before the league title returned to Old Trafford. By then the likes of Allenby Chilton, Jack Rowley, Stanley Pearson and Johnny Carey had moved on but their place in the club's history was assured.

October 1952
A shaky start to the season sees United slip into the bottom half of the table.

November 1952
As results drift and grumbles continue, Matt Busby publicly states that there is a pool of talent soon to come through from the youth side.

May 1952
The Manchester United youth team win the first FA Youth Cup – a trophy they would go on to win five times in a row.

'Manboy' Duncan Edwards was a key figure in Matt Busby's youthful squad.

CHAPTER FIVE

JOY AND TRAGEDY

Matt Busby promised there were great players waiting to come through United's ranks. Over the next few years, his emergent young team justified that faith, becoming one of the most exciting teams English football had seen – until the Munich Air Disaster's cruel intervention...

It says something about the impact of the Busby Babes that nearly half a century later the nickname still evokes all the best traditions of Manchester United – youth, attacking football and, of course, success.

The policy of finding young players and nurturing them into the first team was one that Matt Busby had always had in mind. He wanted to create a team made up of youngsters whom he had taken from school and brought up in what he believed to be the right way.

To help him achieve that goal, he gathered around him a carefully chosen backroom team led by assistant manager Jimmy Murphy whom Busby had met towards the end of the war. A former player, Murphy had made up for any technical deficiencies in his game with guts, spirit and intelligence. In some ways, he was Busby's complete opposite; where Busby was calm, Murphy was fiery, but they made a perfect team.

As Harry Gregg once observed, "Jimmy and Matt together could have climbed Everest. Matt made Jimmy and Jimmy made Matt. They needed each other."

Eventually, Busby brought into the first team all of Jimmy's "Golden Apples" as he called them – he never liked the term "Babes".

But it wasn't just Busby and Murphy who ran what was to prove to be a spectacularly successful youth policy. Bert Whalley looked after the first team and also acted as chief scout. Tom Curry was the first-team trainer and Bill Inglis looked after the second team.

Busby ensured that he had the right people looking for youngsters to pour into these ranks. Joe Armstrong kept an influx of schoolboy talent coming in, particularly from Ireland and Northern Ireland where Billy Behan (Dublin) and Bob Bishop and Bob Harper (Belfast) made sure no potential was overlooked.

The quality of the staff appointed by Busby can be seen in United's dominance of the FA Youth Cup, which they won on five successive occasions from its inception in the 1952/53 season. It can also be seen in the promotion to the first team of so many young players. During 1952/53, Jackie Blanchflower, Bill Foulkes, Dennis Viollet, Jeff Whitefoot, David Pegg, John Doherty and Duncan Edwards were all drafted in on occasion, together with new signing Tommy Taylor.

However, the groundwork for the emergence of the Babes began some years before. From the summer of 1949, Busby intensified the scouting operation and put into place a 'nursery' system to help young players develop. Landladies were interviewed and appointed so as to ensure that the boys who came to United would have something of a home away from home and therefore feel less homesick.

The club acted quickly when they spotted talent. The signings of David Pegg and Duncan Edwards are good examples. Both were playing for England Schoolboys when United became aware of them.

TIMELINE

April 1953 Sixteen-year-old Duncan Edwards makes his debut against Cardiff City at Old Trafford.

August 1953 The 1953/54 season sees the average age of the United side reduce dramatically as seven youth players are drafted in at various stages.

November 1953 Jackie Blanchflower and Dennis Viollet are both on the scoresheet as United trounce Cardiff City 6–1.

MANCHESTER UNITED **OFFICIAL MEMBERS' HISTORY BOOK** 41

Matt Busby moulded a team of real potential including (left to right) Duncan Edwards, Dennis Viollet, Jack Rowley and Bill Foulkes.

Pegg's father, a miner, was determined that his son would not be exploited cheaply. He met every manager who expressed an interest and always asked what they thought of his prospects. Busby, never one to employ hyperbole, merely said, "With reasonable luck, your son will be successful as a professional footballer." The matter-of-fact approach won over Pegg senior and David signed.

Duncan Edwards needed little persuasion. Although the pride of Dudley, the Midlands and England Schoolboy was snatched from under the nose of rivals Wolves.

"I didn't need to 'sell' United to big Duncan," recalled Matt. "As soon as I introduced myself, he said, 'I think Manchester United is the greatest team in the world. I'd give anything to play for you.'"

Edwards, Pegg and the other youngsters, including Roger Byrne, Albert Scanlon and Blanchflower, gave Busby a faith in the future of his team that few on the peripheries of the club could understand. They only saw an ageing first team and were astonished when the manager declared, "There is nothing to panic about. Before long you will see Manchester United back on top."

When the team finished eighth in 1953, it was not the end of an era but the beginning, as Busby's second great team began to take shape. At the time, however, few saw it in that way. In fact, there wasn't a lot of optimism in English football in general. The humiliating defeat of the international team in 1950 by the football novices of the United States was compounded in 1953 and 1954 by 6–3 and 7–1 embarrassments at the hands of the Hungarians.

Typically though, Busby took inspiration from the quality of attacking play displayed by the Eastern Europeans. On a golf course in Scotland during the close season of 1953, he decided that the time had come to bring in some of the youngsters he had nurtured. Jackie Blanchflower, Duncan Edwards, Bill Foulkes and Dennis Viollet were drafted in for the league games against Huddersfield and Arsenal – two games many now declare to be the birth of the Babes, although Roger Byrne, Tommy Taylor and Johnny Berry had already established themselves as first-team players by this stage. Nonetheless, the team was undoubtedly now a predominantly young one, very different from the ageing first XI who had won the title in 1952.

Success did not come overnight. It took a

May 1954 In a period of transition, United finish the season in a creditable fourth place.	**August 1954** Albert Scanlon and Liam Whelan join the young ranks of United first teamers.	**August 1954** Jackie Blanchflower and Dennis Viollet score eight goals between them in United's first four matches of the season.

couple of campaigns before the true potential of the players became apparent. The 1953/54 season ended with United fourth. The next season they were fifth. More youngsters had been introduced, notably Albert Scanlon, Mark Jones and Billy (Liam) Whelan.

The manager's faith was rewarded in the following campaign as his team stormed to championship glory, beating runners-up Blackpool by a margin of 11 points. The average age of the United players that season was 22. The line-up usually read: Wood, Foulkes, Byrne, Whitefoot (to begin with, then Eddie Colman), Jones, Edwards, Berry, Blanchflower (or Doherty or Whelan), Taylor, Viollet and Pegg. The only players still in the team from the title-winning side of four years earlier were Johnny Berry and Roger Byrne.

Byrne, a full-back, had become the cornerstone of the team. He was the first of the Babes to break through and he established himself as a great leader in the process. A superb reader of the game with excellent positional sense, he was always making telling passes that rarely missed their target. Busby once said he never saw Tom Finney or Stanley Matthews have a good game when Byrne was playing opposite them. He was also pretty useful going forward as an attacking overlapping full-back, at a time when the phrase had yet to be coined.

Berry was a right-winger of no little skill who could also poach goals. He quickly secured his place in the team after signing from Birmingham City in 1951.

A number of big names made way for their younger counterparts. John Aston was one, and his reaction showed the esteem in which the manager was held by all at the club.

"Matt Busby had established himself as a far-seeing and shrewd manager," he said. "He had won the respect of all of us which meant that it was easier for him to put over these new ideas. It was very disappointing for the players

Roger Byrne

who had to give way to new men but we were not blind to the fact that the Boss had created a tremendously successful youth team. We accepted the changes because when he said it was for the good of the club, we knew that it was. He treats everyone with respect and in turn is greatly respected. It's this quality which enabled him to move from one successful era to another with a team that became the great Busby Babes."

The team that won the championship in 1956 was indeed made up of great players; young or not, they had all earned their place in the starting line-up.

In goal, Ray Wood made the position his own after initially vying with Jack Crompton and Reg Allen. United had paid Darlington £5,000 for him, aged 18, in 1949. He had previously made just a dozen league appearances. When he didn't get into the first team to begin with, he could be found playing in the A team as a centre-forward.

In front of Wood was Byrne at left-back and Foulkes at right-back. Foulkes, a defensive rock from a mining background, had come to United after being spotted as an amateur with Whiston Boys Club. By 1953, he had established himself in the first team and he went on to become one of the club's longest-serving players, having a spell as captain.

During the 1955/56 season, there was a battle for the right-half position. Jeff Whitefoot started the season there and played enough games to earn a championship medal. A schoolboy international who made his league debut aged 16, he came to United as an office boy and established himself in the first team during the 1953/54 season. A good passer and tackler, it was an indication of the competition for places at United that he couldn't hold on to his first-team berth, which was eventually occupied by Eddie "Snake Hips" Colman.

Some said Colman could send the stand the

May 1955
United finish the season in fifth place but victories over Arsenal, Blackpool and Chelsea hint that things are coming together for Matt Busby.

November 1955
Tommy Taylor (2) and Roger Byrne get the goals as United beat the league champions Chelsea 3–0

December 1955
United go top of the table and celebrate with a run of blistering form, losing just twice in the remainder of the campaign.

MANCHESTER UNITED **OFFICIAL MEMBERS' HISTORY BOOK** 43

wrong way with his shimmy, such was the quality of his deceptive body swerve. This, together with his dazzling dribbles, ball-winning skills and creative ability, made him a favourite of the crowd. Off the pitch, he took a fancy to the Teddy Boy outfits of the day and was a bit of a jiver in his drainpipe trousers and crêpe-soled suede shoes. On the pitch, he struck up an astonishing understanding with Duncan Edwards. Together, these two contributed greatly to the attacking force of the young United team.

The name Duncan Edwards still evokes misty-eyed nostalgia from anyone lucky enough to have seen him play. "The only player who ever made me feel inferior" is how Bobby Charlton described him. Edwards had every attribute needed to become the complete footballer. Speed, power, control, courage – you name it, Edwards had it. Jimmy Murphy had no doubts about just how good the half-back from Dudley was.

"When I used to hear Muhammad Ali proclaim to the world that he was the greatest, I used to smile," said Murphy. "You see, the greatest of them all was an English footballer named Duncan Edwards."

Probably to balance the attacking instincts of Colman and Edwards, Busby put Mark Jones between them at centre-half. A sturdy, dependable stopper, Jones was a bricklayer's apprentice before he joined United. He came through the ranks and made his first league appearance at the age of 17. Having to wait in line for a first-team place behind club captain Allenby Chilton required some patience –

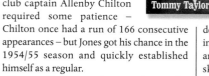

Tommy Taylor

Chilton once had a run of 166 consecutive appearances – but Jones got his chance in the 1954/55 season and quickly established himself as a regular.

Tommy Taylor was by now the regular centre-forward. The "smiling assassin", as he was called by one reporter, always looked as

though he was enjoying his football, a perpetual smile beneath his mop of black hair. Busby signed him from Barnsley in March 1953 for the odd fee of £29,999. Legend has it that Matt gave the spare pound to the tea lady so as not to burden Taylor with a £30,000 tag.

The grandson of a Barnsley player, Taylor had been taken on to the groundstaff at the club straight from school. Later, during his army national service, he sustained a serious knee injury and was discharged. Fortunately, he made a full recovery and as an inside-forward was the target for a number of clubs before Busby's customary charm persuaded him to leave Barnsley. He became an instant success at United at centre-forward with his fierce shot and powerful heading. His apparently endless stamina also enabled him to make countless unselfish runs, creating spaces for his team-mates to exploit.

At inside-left, Dennis Viollet was settled in the first team. A graduate of United's nursery system, he had joined the club at 14 and become a professional at 17. Captain of Manchester Schoolboys and capped five times by England Schoolboys, he made his debut at inside-right during the 1952/53 season, but switched flanks to become one of the club's finest-ever players in a No. 10 shirt.

The inside-right position alternated between Jackie Blanchflower and John Doherty to begin with and then Billy Whelan staked a claim. Jackie Blanchflower's older brother, Danny, was the captain of the Tottenham Hotspur team that won the double in 1961. Jackie, an Irish Schoolboy international, made his league debut at right half-back before moving into the inside-right role. Despite a lack of pace, he was an adaptable and stylish player. Doherty was skilful and thoughtful but plagued by a succession of knee operations that didn't help his chances in what was becoming a very competitive squad.

May 1956
United finish the season as champions, by a margin of 11 points.

August 1956
Liam Whelan scores a hat-trick on the first day of the season as United beat Leicester 3–0.

September 1956
United score 22 goals in their first six matches of the 1956/57 campaign.

Roger Byrne clears the ball in front of keeper Ray Wood and Johnny Carey in an FA Cup third round match against Millwall in January 1953.

David Pegg occupied the left wing for the majority of the campaign. His stream of highly accurate crosses was gratefully pounced on by Taylor and Viollet.

Although the Babes won the 1955/56 championship by 11 points, it wasn't until the turn of the year that their superiority really became apparent. Having gone top of the table in early December, the team moved into top gear, losing just twice in the second half of the season and establishing a winning margin equalled only by Preston, Sunderland and Aston Villa in the previous century. Taylor got the lion's share of the goals, with 25; Viollet and Pegg contributed 20 and nine respectively.

Perhaps most remarkable was Bobby Charlton's contribution, hitting the target 10 times in 14 league appearances. Clearly one for the future, Charlton came in whenever Taylor or Viollet were injured. A miner's son and the nephew of Newcastle great Jackie Milburn, Charlton was to become one of the most popular players in Manchester United's history. He began as an inside-forward but later spent a considerable spell at outside-left where his surging runs and awesome shooting were always a powerful combination. He eventually played at centre-forward for both club and country and was renowned for his

sublime skills and also his consummate professionalism and sportsmanship. The 1955/56 season proved to be just a taste of what was to come from Charlton.

Matt Busby's nursery system had come good. All but three of the title-winning team were home-grown players and it came as little surprise when United went on to repeat their championship success the following season. This time it was Tottenham who finished a distant second, eight points behind the leaders.

The team had altered little over those 12 months, the noticeable changes being Whelan's securing of the inside-right position and the continuing emergence of Bobby Charlton. Whelan's tally of 26 goals was remarkable for an inside-forward whose primary role was to create for others. Billy was a product of the famous Dublin nursery, Home Farm FC, that had served United well over the years. A superb dribbler with tremendous close control, Whelan seemed to glide effortlessly past players as well as having the rather convenient attribute of being a clinical finisher.

It was a high-scoring season all round with Taylor striking 22 times and Viollet on 16 occasions. The championship was taken care of by Easter, and United's final points total of

May 1956
United finish the season as champions again. Their points total of 64 is the highest for 26 years.

August 1956
Dennis Viollet scores a hat-trick as United beat Preston North End 3–2.

September 1956
Anderlecht are Manchester United's first European Cup opponents. The Belgian side are hammered 12–0 on aggregate.

64 was the highest for 26 years.

As well as winning two successive titles, United were making progress in both the European Cup and the FA Cup. The European run was of particular interest as United were the first English team to take part in the competition.

Back in April 1955, the French sports paper *L'Equipe* had arranged a meeting between 16 European clubs, including the English champions Chelsea, to discuss a champions cup. The Football League were not enthusiastic about what they saw as a competition that would intrude on domestic fixtures, and dissuaded Chelsea from taking part. But when United became champions the following season, there was no stopping Matt Busby.

Allegedly, he went to see Stanley Rous of the FA and asked if there was anything in the small print that actually prevented United from entering. Satisfied there wasn't, Busby persuaded the United board to accept the invitation, citing the extra revenue that would be generated for buying floodlights and covering an expanding wage bill. An extra competition also meant more opportunities to utilize all his players. Most of all, though, it was a challenge that the manager just couldn't resist, a chance to prove that United were not only the finest team in the country, but also in Europe. So began his quest for the holy grail, European glory.

Anderlecht were the first opponents in United's inaugural European Cup run of 1956/57. Two legs later, Busby's youngsters had scored a dozen goals and the Anderlecht captain Jeff Mermans admitted, "It was an education. They should pick this whole team for England."

Borussia Dortmund were next. A 3–2 victory took United to the quarter-finals and a meeting with Atletico Bilbao. In the first leg, after falling 3–0 behind, United staged a recovery but the final score was 5–3 to Bilbao.

There was certainly plenty for United to do in the second leg but, not for the first time under Busby, the team responded to the challenge. Berry, Taylor and Viollet got the goals in a match one newspaper described as "the greatest victory in soccer history".

The scene was set for an encounter with Real Madrid, winners of the inaugural European Cup the previous year. United's run in the competition at their first attempt had already captured the imagination of the public and cemented the reputation of the Busby Babes as the most exciting English football team in living memory. The first leg in Madrid was a passionate affair with Real running out 3–1 winners. The return match – the first floodlit European night at Old Trafford – was, if anything, even more heated than the first. A 2–2 draw wasn't enough to keep United in the competition but the fans' appetite had been whetted. The European obsession was growing.

On the domestic front, there was further excitement when United put together an FA Cup run that took them all the way to the final. With the league already won, an historic double was up for grabs. Aston Villa stood in the way.

Busby later admitted that on the morning of the match, he had never been more sure of

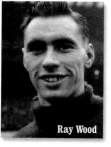

Ray Wood

victory in his footballing career, but he hadn't foreseen the controversy that was to follow.

Six minutes into the match at Wembley, Ray Wood collected a header from Villa's Peter McParland and was about to kick it clear. But McParland continued his run and charged into the keeper, shattering Wood's cheekbone. Even in the days of little protection for goalkeepers, it was an outrageous challenge and Wood had to be carried off the field.

United struggled on, holding Villa to a scoreless first half. No substitutions were allowed and Jackie Blanchflower took over in goal, Wood bravely playing on in the wing position to make up the numbers although he

October 1956 Bobby Charlton makes his league debut aged 18 against Charlton Athletic, scoring twice.

December 1956 Duncan Edwards scores his only home goal of the season in the 3–1 victory over Luton.

April 1957 Old Trafford hosts its first floodlit European night, a 2–2 draw between United and Real Madrid that sees the Spanish giants win 5–3 on aggregate.

was little more than a passenger. The team had lost their balance and Villa exploited this in the second half, McParland scoring twice to add insult to injury. Taylor pulled one back and, in the final minutes, Wood went back in goal but it was not United's day.

The 1957/58 season began brightly and then around Christmas, United went on a seven-match unbeaten run including a 4–0 thrashing of Leicester City. The game marked the debut of new signing Harry Gregg for whom Busby paid Doncaster Rovers £23,500. It was a record fee for a goalkeeper and showed once again that Busby was not afraid to spend money when he felt it was necessary.

The manager planned to make full use of the players at his disposal with a triple assault on the league, FA Cup and Europe. By the turn of the year, everything was going to plan. United were in good shape in the league, had reached the fifth round of the Cup and were in the quarter-finals of the European Cup.

The first leg of the quarter-final was against Red Star Belgrade and ended in a 2–1 home win. Before the return, two league encounters took place. The first was a 7–2 win over Bolton

that included a Bobby Charlton hat-trick. The second was a trip to Highbury that turned out to be the Babes' last match on English soil. It lives in the memory of all lucky enough to have witnessed it.

United were three up before half-time and victory seemed assured. But in the second half the home team staged a tremendous recovery to level the scores.

Any thoughts that the visitors would settle for a draw were quickly dispelled. The visitors pushed forward looking for a winner. Scanlon and Charlton combined to provide Viollet with United's fourth and then Taylor grabbed his second and United's fifth. But the drama wasn't over yet. Derek Tapscott slipped through United's tired defence to ensure the game finished on a knife-edge. United held on for an epic 5–4 victory. When the referee blew for time, the players collapsed in each other's arms. Supporters knew they had witnessed a magnificent game that had confirmed the Babes as the most exhilarating team of their generation. It was a fitting testament.

After that footballing exhibition, United prepared to make the trip to Belgrade and

May 1957
Ray Woods is charged into by Aston Villa's Peter McParland in the FA Cup Final and 10-man United lose 2–1.

September 1957
United thrash Leeds 5–0 at Old Trafford.

September 1957
For the fifth time in six weeks United score four or more goals in a game as they beat Aston Villa 4–1.

MANCHESTER UNITED **OFFICIAL MEMBERS' HISTORY BOOK**   **47**

attention turned to the task ahead. Could United defend their slim one-goal advantage?

An answer seemed to be provided 90 seconds into the match when Viollet gave United a 1–0 lead. Charlton added two more and victory seemed assured. Of course, this being United there had to be more drama. Red Star struck twice, sending the crowd into a frenzy. Still United continued to attack but Red Star were the next to score. A precise free-kick from Kostic eluded Gregg's fingertips and the game was level at 3–3. Despite further incidents at both ends, that was the way it finished and United were through, 5–4 aggregate winners.

After the match there was a formal ceremony and banquet before the night dissipated into rather less formal drinks and card games. The next morning everyone was in good spirits as they prepared for the flight home, via a refuelling stop in Munich, and a potentially title-deciding clash with Wolves.

But the team didn't get home, not that day, and some of them not at all. In the February snow and ice of Munich, the second great team built by Matt Busby came to a premature end.

The plane crash at Munich on 6 February 1958, which claimed the lives of 21 people including eight United players and three staff, left an indelible mark on the history of Manchester United Football Club.

Duncan Edwards, Roger Byrne, Eddie Colman, Mark Jones, David Pegg, Tommy Taylor, Billy Whelan and Geoff Bent (average age 24) all perished. The dead also included United coach Bert Whalley, trainer Tom Curry, club secretary Walter Crickmer and eight British journalists. It was both a football and human tragedy of immense proportions.

The team's ill-fated visit to Munich was a scheduled refuelling stop on the way back from Belgrade but from the beginning nothing went to plan. On arrival at Belgrade airport, Johnny Berry couldn't find his passport and the flight was delayed. Eventually an immigration officer decided to unload the luggage from the plane's hold and they found Berry's passport in his suitcase.

The weather was murky and visibility was poor when the players finally boarded Flight 609 in mid-morning. However, Captain James Thain at the controls of the Elizabethan Class G–ALZU AS 57 Lord Burghley, with his co-pilot and friend Captain Kenneth Rayment alongside, made a smooth take-off and everything seemed to be going to plan.

6 February 1958: the sickening aftermath of the Munich air crash that claimed 21 lives.

TIMELINE

December 1957	January 1958	January 1958
Harry Gregg signs for United. The fee of £23,500 is a record fee for a goalkeeper.	Manchester United beat Red Star Belgrade 2–1 in the first leg of their European Cup quarter-final tie.	Bobby Charlton scores a hat-trick as United demolish Bolton 7–2.

Following a short fuel stop, they expected to arrive back in Manchester by teatime. But as they landed in Munich, snow was already falling. Refuelling took less than 20 minutes and by 2 pm the pilots were ready to take off again and continue their way to Manchester. Captain Rayment took over the controls and at 2.31 pm clearance was given for take-off, but he abandoned the attempt when the engines sounded an uneven note. He wasn't unduly worried because this 'boost surging' was not unusual for Elizabethan planes. Rayment tried again at 2.34, but had the same problem. The pilots agreed to taxi the plane back to the airport terminal for further investigation.

The players disembarked and passed the time waiting for the departure call buying presents and cigarettes. With the weather deteriorating, Duncan Edwards sent a telegram to his landlady in Manchester which read: ALL FLIGHTS CANCELLED – STOP – FLYING TOMORROW – STOP – DUNCAN.

Soon though, they were called back on the plane. It started off down the runway, but then someone shouted that Alf Clarke, a journalist for the *Manchester Evening Chronicle*, was missing. The plane rumbled back to the terminal yet again and Clarke (who would be fatally injured minutes later) got a lot of light-hearted stick from fellow hacks when he belatedly appeared.

Seconds later, the pilots made their third attempt to take off and it went horribly wrong. The Lord Burghley careered off the runway and skidded across a road towards a residential area. The left wing and part of the tail were wrenched off on impact with a house, the cockpit ploughed into a tree and the fuselage crashed into a wooden hut containing a fuel-loaded truck which exploded into a fireball.

Goalkeeper Harry Gregg vividly remembers the screeching and banging as the plane spun out of control and then the eerie silence when it finally came to a halt. "There was no screaming or shouting. It was pitch black and I thought, 'I'm dead, I'm in hell.'"

The tragic news reaches England.

Gregg realized he was alive only when he felt blood trickling down his forehead and saw daylight and flames above him. As he kicked his way out of the wreckage, one of the pilots, James Thain (Kenneth Rayment died later in hospital), came past and urged him to run away. But Gregg heard a baby crying and went back into the wreckage, ignoring the explosions all around him.

His heroism saved the life of the baby, the child's mother and numerous colleagues. Even though Gregg thought Bobby Charlton and Dennis Viollet were dead he dragged their bodies clear and both survived. He also helped Matt Busby, who'd suffered punctured lungs and broken leg bones, and Jackie Blanchflower, who was lying badly injured with Roger Byrne's dead body on top of him.

Eventually, vehicles arrived at the desolate scene and the injured and dead were rushed to Munich's Rechts Der Isar hospital. Three of United's party – Matt Busby, Johnny Berry and Duncan Edwards – were fighting for their lives. The last rites were twice administered to Matt Busby, but he pulled through and returned to Manchester 71 days later. Berry survived although his football career was over. Edwards fought bravely for 15 days, but finally died of kidney failure.

On the night of the disaster, Harry Gregg asked James Thain why the take-off had failed. "He told me about Velocity One, when you have to lift the undercarriage off the ground. He said that point of no return had been reached."

There was no going back for United either. The club would never be the same again.

February 1958
1 February: the Busby Babes play their last match on British soil – a stunning 5–4 victory over Arsenal at Highbury.

February 1958
5 February: United draw 3–3 with Red Star Belgrade in the second leg of their quarter-final, winning on aggregate 5–4.

February 1958
6 February: the Munich air disaster claims the life of 21 people including eight Manchester United players and three staff.

MANCHESTER UNITED **OFFICIAL MEMBERS' HISTORY BOOK**   49

Matt Busby's injuries meant he had to watch the 1958 World Cup at home rather than from the Scotland manager's seat.

CHAPTER SIX

A STEADY RECOVERY

Matt Busby predicted it would take five years for Manchester United to fully recover from the tragedy of Munich. As usual, his prediction wasn't far from the truth as the club slowly recuperated...

Matt Busby's slow and painful recuperation continued during the summer of 1958, depriving him of the chance to add an intriguing new dimension to his managerial career.

In January, with Scotland having qualified for that summer's World Cup in Sweden, he had accepted his country's invitation to be their team manager for the tournament. Busby's ambition and confidence had led him to declare at the time of his appointment, "I aim not to have a team content merely to put up a respectable show, but one that will take the field with the aim of winning the global trophy." It was not to be. Post-Munich, Busby was not fit enough for the stresses of such a job and he had to watch on television as his country exited at the group stage.

The tournament still had a considerable influence on Busby. As he watched the black and white images at his home in Kings Road, Chorlton, during those June weeks, he enthused about the attacking play of Didi and Garrincha of Brazil, Lennart Skoglund of Sweden and Just Fontaine of France, the man who set the all-time World Cup scoring record of 13 goals at the tournament. Watching the first World Cup to be televised was, as he put it, "more education!" It also helped to rekindle his fascination with the game as it was played outside the British Isles. Busby's belief in European competition had been shaken by the Munich disaster but watching that World Cup helped cement his desire to build a new United team capable of competing in Europe.

He almost had the chance to take United into the European Cup straightaway, despite the club having finished ninth in the First Division at the end of the 1957/58 season. In the aftermath of the Munich disaster, which had generated sympathy around Europe, the club received a generous invitation from the European Cup's ruling body to enter the 1958/59 tournament. The FA gave their consent but the Football League did not. United went to the Football League's board of appeal who upheld United's right to accept the invitation but the League then went to the joint FA and League Consultative Committee who denied United entry to the European Cup on the grounds that, as it was a tournament for champion clubs, they were not qualified to enter.

Leaving aside the fact that some of the clubs who entered the competition in those early days were not actually champions of their countries, the League's determination to thwart United looked like revenge for Busby's hurdling of their opposition two years earlier.

United began the 1958/59 league season in style, with Bobby Charlton collecting a hat-trick in a 5–2 opening-day thrashing of Chelsea at Old Trafford. Albert Scanlon was back on the left wing for that match, having made a successful recovery from the head and leg injuries he had sustained in the crash. He was to be an ever-present over the season, scoring 16 goals. Half-back Fred Goodwin was the only other United player to appear in every one of the club's matches that season. Wilf

TIMELINE

May 1958
A grieving United team, full of reserves and youth players, pour their energies into an FA Cup run and reach the final before losing to Bolton 2-0.

May 1958
United play their European Cup semi-final against AC Milan and exit the competition after a 5–2 aggregate defeat.

June 1958
The World Cup takes place in Sweden. A recuperating Matt Busby is not well enough to travel with Scotland.

MANCHESTER UNITED **OFFICIAL MEMBERS' HISTORY BOOK**   51

The first Manchester United team group photo after Munich (left to right): Front Row: Jack Crompton, (trainer) Alec Dawson, Mark Pearson, Billy Foulkes (captain), Ernie Taylor, Colin Webster, and Bill Inglis (assistant trainer). Back Row: Bobby Harrop, Ian Greaves, Fred Goodwin, Harry Gregg, Stan Crowther, Ron Cope and Shay Brennan.

McGuinness, only 20 years old but a first-team regular since Munich, played in all but three of United's matches. His appetite for hard work in midfield was of enormous benefit. He held together the reshaped team and helped it gel.

Centre-forward Dennis Viollet shared 50 league goals with Charlton, who became fully established as a first-team regular. Still only 20, the youngster was suddenly the focal point of the United side. "The Munich air disaster came at a time when I was trying to establish myself in a regular first-team position with Manchester United," he commented in 1961. "I seemed to become a sort of symbol, particularly with youngsters, of the new United. Simultaneously, it was urged I should be given an England place. I am naturally shy and all this confused me; too many people were making too much fuss."

Charlton and Viollet were joined in the forward line by Albert Quixall, whom Busby made a British record signing when he paid Sheffield Wednesday £45,000 for him – £10,000 more than the previous British record – in September 1958. Quixall was a skilful, creative inside-forward but something of a luxury player. He was at his best when United were well on top in a game but less effective in adversity. He managed just four goals in his debut season.

There was no European competition to distract the players from the league and a surprise 3–0 third-round FA Cup defeat at Third Division Norwich City ensured that the First Division remained central to everyone's thoughts. The club played the absolute minimum of matches necessary – 43 in all. That lack of fixture congestion was a major boon and progress was such that a 2–1 win over Wolverhampton Wanderers in February 1959 brought United level with the Midlands club at the top of the table. However, United lost three of their last 12 games and finished second to Wolves, six points behind the champions. Amid the disappointment at missing out on the title there was satisfaction and surprise that the first full season after Munich had gone so well.

The Stretford End was covered in the summer of 1959, increasing the comfort of the thousands who stood there, and at the start of the season optimism ran high that there would also be progress on the pitch. The opening game delivered a clue as to how United would

July 1958
The Football League denies United the chance to compete in the 1958/59 European Cup despite an invitation from the tournament's ruling body.

August 1958
Bobby Charlton scores a hat-trick on the opening day of the season as United defeat Chelsea 5–2 at Old Trafford.

September 1958
Albert Quixall signs for Manchester United from Sheffield Wednesday for a British record fee of £45,000.

fare. Dennis Viollet scored twice in the match at West Bromwich Albion but United ended it 3–2 losers. Between then and the final fixture of the season, Viollet scored another 30 times, giving him a total of 32 league goals for the 1959/60 season. It remains the league scoring record for a United player. Viollet missed six matches so his tally averaged out at almost a goal a game.

Although Viollet and Charlton once again shared a total of 50 goals, as they had the previous season, the team proved less consistent overall. Convincing wins would be followed by hefty defeats and vice versa. This inconsistency continued right up until the closing fixtures, with United beating West Ham 5–3, then losing 5–2 to Arsenal before defeating Everton 5–0 in the final league match of the season. Despite such volatile fluctuations in their results, United still managed to finish in seventh place in the First Division. They had scored 102 goals over the season, just one short of the tally of the 1956/57 championship-winning team. They had, however, conceded the not so grand total of 80.

Matt Busby had made it clear that it would take a full five years for United to recover from the crash and, as so often, his words were ringing true, despite the optimism that had been generated by United's stirring finale the previous season. Thoughts of the crash were still never far away even two years on and on a rainy day in late February 1960 Matt Busby unveiled the Munich memorial plaque in honour of all those who had lost their lives in the crash.

In a poor start to the 1960/61 season, United haemorrhaged goals, leaving them third from bottom of the First Division at the beginning of October. Busby quickly took steps to remedy the situation. Shay Brennan was pulled back from midfield to right-back. A player who combined a highly disciplined approach to his

Albert Quixall

duties to the team with fine ball-playing skills, he was the ideal full-back for Busby. Bill Foulkes switched to centre-half, a position in which the rugged ex-miner appeared born to play. They were joined in November 1960 by Irishman Noel Cantwell for whom Busby paid West Ham United £29,500, making him Britain's most expensive full-back.

Johnny Giles, an 18-year-old Irishman, became a regular in midfield over the season. He was joined there by two other well-loved youngsters – 18-year-old Nobby Stiles and Jimmy Nicholson, a well-built, skilled 17-year-old from Belfast whom the crowd immediately took to their hearts. Both were fortunate enough to be part of the United side that played host to Real Madrid in a friendly match that October of 1960.

While United struggled in the league, this glamorous fixture was a pleasant reminder to the Old Trafford faithful of the joys of European football. The president of Real, Santiago Bernabeu, had met Matt Busby in Madrid and had told him that, in sympathy with United for the Munich crash, he would waive his club's usual fee for friendlies whenever Busby wished to bring the five-times European champions to Old Trafford. A crowd of 51,000 watched enthralled that autumn night as Real, led by the magnificent Alfredo Di Stefano, won 3–2. United's goals were scored by inside-left Mark Pearson and Nicholson. It was a reminder to all of the glamour involved in floodlit European games, those nights when the green rectangle of the footballing stage, the focus of so many lives, was lit up by the colour of cosmopolitan talents.

That inspirational night helped spur United on in the League for the remainder of the year and by the time they faced Manchester City at Old Trafford on New Year's Eve they had moved into the top half of the table. It proved to be a fond farewell to 1960 – in the 5–1 win

Noel Cantwell takes the field.

Alex Dawson netted the first hat-trick in a Manchester derby since October 1921 when the great Joe Spence had scored all three goals for United in their 3–1 win.

Busby was aware that United were still far from the finished article but that year he mused, "I should like to see the honours in England won by a pure footballing side, the sort of team that concentrates on ball skills above all else. Such a team could inspire the other 91 clubs. But for the air disaster, I like to feel that others would now be copying United to the benefit of the whole league."

United suffered a serious blow when goalkeeper Harry Gregg badly damaged his shoulder against Spurs in January 1961. With substitutes still not yet allowed under Football Association rules, Dawson replaced him in goal. Gregg, with his shoulder strapped up, took Dawson's place at centre-forward and it was Gregg, bizarrely, who played a decisive role in United's winning goal. His natty backheel set up Pearson to make the final score 2–0.

The combination of firm defensive football and clever attacking evident in that game had been encouraging but the optimism was short-lived. United immediately suffered their most severe defeat of the season, going down 6–0 away to Leicester City. Ronnie Briggs, a 17 year-old from Belfast, made his debut in goal in that game and his confidence was shattered further when United took on Sheffield Wednesday in the fourth round of the FA Cup the following week. After a 1–1 draw at Hillsborough, the two sides met in the replay at Old Trafford four days later. Goalkeeping errors by Briggs allowed Wednesday to take a 4–1 lead by half-time and they eventually ran out 7–2 victors.

Briggs returned to the reserves and Mike Pinner, a 26-year-old amateur and law graduate from Cambridge University, was signed from QPR in February 1961 as Busby reacted to his goalkeeping emergency. Pinner and 20-year-old David Gaskell shared goalkeeping duties in the absence of the incapacitated Gregg.

United participated in the Football League Cup, then in its first year. A second-round defeat at Bradford City in October 1960 ended their interest in the tournament, then treated very much as a minor affair by the bigger clubs and their supporters. It would be six years before United played in that competition again.

The 1960/61 season ended with United in seventh place for the second successive year, a commendable effort after their sluggish start. Bobby Charlton was United's top scorer, despite having been moved from inside-left to the left wing. The player preferred the inside-forward position but his pace and precision made him an excellent winger.

"I would still eventually like to return to an inside-forward position, should the Boss come to think me sufficiently mature," said Charlton. "Inside, you're more in the game for longer spells. It gives more satisfaction. You are less likely to let your mind wander and lose that all-important concentration."

Charlton was joined in the forward line for the 1961/62 season by David Herd, a 28-year-old Scottish international centre-forward who was purchased from Arsenal for a fee of £35,000. Busby had played alongside

August 1959
Dennis Viollet scores twice in the opening game of the 1959/60 season. He would go on to score a club record 32 league goals.

December 1959
Wilf McGuinness is forced to retire from the game after a severe leg break.

February 1960
Matt Busby unveils the Munich memorial plaque to commemorate those who died in the air disaster.

Herd's father Alec, an inside-forward, at Manchester City in the Thirties. David too had played alongside his father for Stockport County before moving to Highbury. Herd had been Arsenal's top scorer for four successive seasons yet, puzzlingly, the Arsenal manager, George Swindin, had tried to sell the player on numerous occasions. A few months earlier, Swindin attempted to arrange a move to Huddersfield Town for Herd in part-exchange for Huddersfield forward Denis Law. Herd had scored 30 league and FA Cup goals for Arsenal in the 1960/61 season. A fearsome right foot combined with a hearty appetite for the game made him an exciting capture.

With a surplus of forwards at the club, Dennis Viollet was subsequently sold to Stoke City in January 1962 for £22,000. There he joined up with Stanley Matthews who decades later compared Viollet to Teddy Sheringham for his deft touches and underrated contributions to the team.

The young Bobby Charlton.

United were among the favourites for the 1961/62 championship but despite a good start, a disastrous run of results in the autumn torpedoed their championship chances. From a place in the leading pack of clubs, United tumbled towards the relegation zone. By Christmas they were second to bottom but the now usual rally in the second half of the season took them clear of the drop and into a final position of 15th. It was the club's lowest finish since Busby had become manager.

The Cup produced better cheer. A win over Bolton Wanderers in the third round was followed by a stylish victory over Arsenal. Freakishly, the fifth round produced yet another FA Cup tie with Sheffield Wednesday, but this time after replays in that match and in a quarter-final with Preston North End, United found themselves in the semi-finals. There their luck ran out and they were outclassed by opponents Tottenham Hotspur, the holders of the trophy. The match at neutral Hillsborough finished 3–1 in the Londoners' favour.

Busby now seemed generally happy with his defence and midfield. One of the few changes

to those sections of his team was the introduction of Tony Dunne as a regular in the left-back position, which he shared with fellow Irishman Noel Cantwell during 1961/62. The manager was less happy with his side's attacking qualities, constantly chopping and changing his front players to little avail. Herd scored 17 times but, overall, goals were scarce – Quixall and Charlton only just made it into double figures.

Drastic measures were required if United were to become a consistently strong force in English football once again. Busby's attempts at bringing through youngsters had been partially successful and it was always his preference to mould a player into the right type for Manchester United. Despite that, if the right player was available to buy, the United manager was not averse to purchasing talent and in the summer of 1962, when Scottish international forward Denis Law became available, Busby did not hesitate to dip deep into the Old Trafford coffers to find the necessary transfer fee.

Busby had been keeping an eye on Law ever since the mid-Fifties when the player had joined Huddersfield Town as an amateur.

May 1960
After a high-scoring (but also high-conceding) season, United finish in seventh place.

November 1960
'Britain's most expensive full-back', Irishman Noel Cantwell joins United from West Ham for £29,000.

December 1960
Alex Dawson scores a hat-trick as United beat Manchester City 5–1.

MANCHESTER UNITED **OFFICIAL MEMBERS' HISTORY BOOK**   55

"When we were losing 2–0 at half-time in a youth match at Heckmondwike, I wondered who was taking us apart," Busby recalled. "Then I realized it was a little will-o'-the-wisp called Law, who had scored both goals. I knew then that Huddersfield had found someone more than a bit special."

By the early 1960s, Law had become a fully fledged goalscorer of the highest calibre with Manchester City and in 1961 his talents had taken him to Torino in Italy. A new British record fee of £115,000 secured his return to Manchester a year later. It also put United in debt for the first time in the Busby era.

The United attack had a more settled look in the 1962/63 season. Law took his place at inside-left with Charlton outside him on the wing. On the other flank, Johnny Giles was on the right wing, with Quixall inside him. Herd was at centre-forward. Law's debut for United, a home league match with West Bromwich Albion in August 1962, began with a flourish. After 90 seconds, Stiles slipped a pass into the path of Herd whose shot went darting into the net. Five minutes later, Johnny Giles took a pass from Brennan and curved a cross into the heart of the penalty area. Law, under pressure in the air, got in front of his defender to glance the ball into the far corner of the net. That was as good as it got for United on the day. Unable to add to their 2–0 lead, West Brom pegged them back with two late goals for a draw and the United players were slow-handclapped by their own supporters in the latter stages of the match.

Throughout the season, rich entertainment alternated with lapses of on-field discipline that undid the team's constructive work. A series of patchy performances caused United to plummet to the foot of the table and by mid-May they were in grave danger of relegation. Their third-last fixture took them to Maine Road to face a City side that was in a similar predicament. This

game would decide which Manchester outfit would join Leyton Orient in demotion to the Second Division.

United had three matches remaining while City had just two. United also had one point more than their rivals. It looked ominous for United when Alex Harley's strike put City ahead after eight minutes and City were still 1–0 up as the match entered its final stages. Then David Wagstaffe, City's outside-left, was short with a long-range backpass to his goalkeeper Harry Dowd. Law was on to it in a flash and as he reached the penalty area, Dowd appeared to grab his ankles. The two opponents tumbled to the ground in a ball of confusion. The referee decided it was a penalty, Albert Quixall netted and United emerged with a somewhat fortunate draw. United's 3–1 defeat of Leyton Orient at Old Trafford three days later sent City down.

Despite the team's troubles, Busby had kept his nerve, kept confidence in his players and had maintained a largely settled side. The only notable addition to the team during the season had been Pat Crerand, a midfielder signed from Celtic in February for a fee of £56,000. As with Law, when the player had become available, Busby hadn't hesitated to swoop. Crerand added real finesse to the midfield.

One of the most severe winters in history had frozen Britain in early 1963, leading to a two-month mid-season hiatus. United went from late December 1962 to late February 1963 without a match. It meant that the FA Cup did not begin until March and United compressed four FA Cup ties into that month, defeating Huddersfield Town in the third round, then knocking out Aston Villa and Chelsea, before ending March with a quarter-final victory over Coventry City. The semi-final with Second Division Southampton was a dour affair that was settled when Denis Law scraped the ball over the Southampton line midway through

Denis Law

TIMELINE

January 1961
United suffer their worst league defeat of the season – a 6–0 thrashing by Leicester City.

February 1961
Sheffield Wednesday storm to a 7–2 victory as Manchester United make an ignominious fourth-round exit from the FA Cup.

July 1961
David Herd signs for United from Arsenal. He would go on to score 144 goals in 262 appearances.

56   MANCHESTER UNITED OFFICIAL MEMBERS' HISTORY BOOK

"It went just as we had planned it": United celebrate the 3–1 1963 FA Cup victory over Leicester City

the first half. It was enough to take the club into their fourth FA Cup final under Busby.

Manchester United were the most unlikely of FA Cup final underdogs – they were by far the most expensively assembled side ever to have reached that stage of the competition. That was counterbalanced by the fact that they had only just escaped relegation days before. Their opponents Leicester City, in contrast, had finished the season in fourth place.

It was the Football Association's centenary year and the 1963 Cup final was a fitting celebration of that sporting body's great tournament. Freed of the drudgery of keeping the club free of relegation, United's players revelled in the occasion and controlled the match from the start, taking the lead after half an hour through Denis Law.

Collecting Pat Crerand's centre, Law tamed the ball with his left then cleverly shielded it as he turned with his back to goal, wrong-footing two defenders as he did so. That calculated movement opened up the whole target for him and allowed him to hit a swift but highly controlled shot on the turn past Banks.

David Herd added a second for United before Leicester retaliated through Ken Keyworth's fine diving header. But with five minutes of the match remaining, Herd struck again to ensure victory.

"It went just as we had planned it," said Busby afterwards. On the team's return to Manchester more than 300,000 people lined the streets to welcome their heroes home. The United players were astonished at the crowds. Busby had stood by his men throughout a testing season and his loyalty had been rewarded by his players' performances at Wembley. The manager had stated that it would take five years for the club to recover from Munich and, as in so many matters, he had been proved correct.

"Our supporters have helped considerably in our success," Busby commented in the minutes after the Cup final. "I want them to share in it and to reassure them about our future. I believe that it will be a bright one."

Manchester United's rehabilitation was complete. The club could now look to the future with confidence.

May 1962
From a relegation spot at Christmas, United rally somewhat to finish 15th in the table.

July 1962
A British record fee of £115,000 brings Denis Law to Manchester United.

May 1963
Manchester United win the FA Cup final, defeating Leicester 3–1.

With Bobby Charlton, George
Best and Denis Law formed a
formidable attacking trio

CHAPTER SEVEN

A DREAM FULFILLED

Denis Law, George Best and Bobby Charlton: three outstanding talents blended together in the Sixties to lead the way in creating a decade of delight at Old Trafford and European triumph for Matt Busby...

Fast, flowing, attacking football was always the central concern of Manchester United's three most famous players of the Sixties – Denis Law, George Best and Bobby Charlton. All three were obsessed with driving play forward, getting goals and overwhelming opponents through their sheer desire to win matches in the most stylish manner possible. That commitment to entertaining football won the club thousands of new fans as the Sixties progressed because more and more teams were adopting a defensive guise as a means of sneaking off with results. That was never United's way. They had to play to the strengths of their key performers and that meant the entire team was oriented towards attack.

Law, Best and Charlton were world-class talents, each of whose attacking skills on their own would have lit up any club. That all three came together at Old Trafford was fortunate for the club's followers, but it was no accident – they were the type of players that Matt Busby had devoted his life to encouraging and nurturing for Manchester United. At the outset of the Sixties he had made clear his commitment to entertaining football in the face of the increasing functionalism that was disfiguring the face of the English game.

"We are breeding a number of teams whose outlook seems to be that pace, punch and fitness are all that is required to win all the honours in the game," he commented. "They forget that without pure skills these virtues count for precisely nothing."

As the 1963/64 season began, Law and Charlton were firm fixtures in United's array of starts, especially after their contribution to the FA Cup win the previous May, the club's first trophy in six years. That spring had also been a momentous time in the life of George Best. He had been on the United groundstaff since August 1961 but on 22 May 1963, three days before United's Wembley win, he turned 17 and was offered professional terms by Busby.

The gifted teenager from Northern Ireland was soon ready for first-team football and was given his debut in a 1–0 home win over West Bromwich Albion on 14 September 1963. Law was missing through injury that day and afterwards Best returned to the youth team. It was more than three months before Busby judged the time was right to have Best back in the first team, for a match with Burnley on 28 December. Law was missing from the line-up again. The FA had suspended him for 28 days on 5 December after he had been sent off against Aston Villa in mid-November. By the time Law was ready to return, for a home match against Birmingham City on 11 January, Charlton was missing through injury.

It meant that the trio's initial first-team appearance together was in an away match against West Brom on 18 January 1964. United lined up with Charlton at centre-forward – this was the season in which Bobby Charlton finally got his wish and moved from the left wing to a more central role – Law at inside-left and Best on the left wing. From the start, they were a success, blending together beautifully.

TIMELINE

September 1963
George Best makes his United debut in a 1–0 home win against West Bromwich Albion.

January 1964
The match against West Bromwich Albion is the first instance of Best, Law and Charlton all being in the United starting line-up. All three also score in a 4–1 win.

October 1964
Denis Law scores a hat-trick as United beat Willem 7–2 on aggregate in the European Cup-Winners' Cup.

The original King of Old Trafford, Denis Law.

positive approach to football. They were among the challengers for the league title, they were defending the FA Cup and they were managing that rare trick of blending instinctive individualism with teamwork.

They were also back in Europe after a five-season absence, much to Matt Busby's joy. "Once again we will be able to bring inter-continental football to Manchester," the United manager had said in the immediate aftermath of the 1963 FA Cup win over Leicester, "and this is something I am personally delighted about. Over the years this has always been a major objective for United. I fervently believe that only by meeting the great sides of Europe can we hope to improve our game in this country. This is something we must aim at, for British football needs the impetus, at club and international level, which competitive football against other European sides will provide."

While Busby remained a man who could be entranced by the romance of football, he also had the necessary core of steel required by any manager. At the beginning of that 1963/64 season, Johnny Giles, a good prospect for the future, had been transferred to Leeds United for £37,500 after one disagreement too many with Busby. It hardly seemed to matter at the time because the club had young talent aplenty; Ian Moir took over from Giles at outside-right while David Sadler, a 17-year-old whose signature had been sought by almost every First Division club, made his debut as a centre-forward in August, and the club soon topped the First Division.

It was as league leaders that they travelled to Holland for their opening European Cup Winners' Cup tie with Willem II Tilburg in late September. Harry Gregg and Bill Foulkes were the only players in the side who had also been involved in United's last European tie, with Milan in 1958, although Munich survivor Bobby Charlton was also in the line-up. It was an unhappy night for United. They went 1–0 behind to the part-timers although David Herd quickly equalized. The return at Old Trafford

They scored all four of the goals in United's 4–1 win that day, Law hitting the net twice and Best and Charlton once each. Best's goal was his second for United, but while his first for the club had been a straightforward strike this one was of the type that would establish his reputation as master of the unexpected. Taking a clever pass from Law, Best went skating across the slippery surface, flitting wide of the West Brom defenders, shaking them off but simultaneously reducing the angle at which he could shoot at goal. With his opponents baffled, Best swiftly swiped the ball into the tiniest space inside the post to score United's second goal of the game.

United were now proving the benefits of a

November 1963	December 1963	February 1964
Harry Gregg suffers a broken collarbone in a clash with Liverpool's Ron Yeats.	United defeat title rivals Tottenham in the Cup-Winners Cup 4–3 on aggregate.	Denis Law scores another European hat-trick as United defeat Sporting Lisbon 4-1 at Old Trafford. But Lisbon win the return to go through 6-4 on aggregate.

three weeks later was much more encouraging, United streaking to a 6–1 win that included a spectacular hat-trick from Denis Law.

The next round promised to be much more testing. United were drawn against the holders, Tottenham Hotspur, who in May 1963 had become the first British club to win a European trophy. This tie was given an additional edge since Spurs and United had both taken turns at leading the First Division.

The first leg, at White Hart Lane, finished 2–0 to the hosts. Six days later in the return at Old Trafford, United were in storming form, quickly wiping out the 2–0 deficit through a double from Herd. Jimmy Greaves put Spurs ahead again on aggregate and within minutes the match became 10-a-side when Maurice Setters had to leave the field with blood pouring from a head wound; Spurs midfielder Dave Mackay had been carried off the pitch with a broken leg in the first-half.

United now drew on all their resources. Charlton sent a shot whistling over the crossbar, but when Crerand sent a pass into his path with 10 minutes remaining, he found the target. With seconds to go and Tottenham on the back foot, Crerand and Charlton produced a replica of that goal, Crerand slipping the ball down the inside-right channel and Charlton making no mistake from close range. Even though it had been a tie between two English clubs, the match had produced the type of drama and excitement Busby always anticipated from European competition.

The quarter-finals threw up a tie with Sporting Lisbon and 60,000 United fans went home from Old Trafford delighted with a 4–1 win in the first leg. The Portuguese had keenly disputed both the United spot-kicks awarded that night, but Sporting got one of their own after two minutes of the second leg and Osvaldo scored from the spot. Ten minutes

Bobby Charlton

later the same player poked the ball into the United net from close range.

With Sporting moving the ball around at whirlwind speed and incessantly running off the ball swiftly and surely, United were in trouble. Portuguese pressure told once again shortly after half-time when Geo levelled the aggregate score. That inspired his side to make a final push for the winner in the second half. Morais made it 4–0 on the night, then Osvaldo finished it off with a 35-yard free-kick that streaked past Gaskell. Not only were United out of Europe, the 5–0 reverse was the club's heaviest defeat in European competition.

Either side of that match in Lisbon on 18 March 1964, the club's chances of winning a domestic trophy had disappeared. An FA Cup semi-final with West Ham United had resulted in a 3–1 defeat and when they lost 3–0 at Liverpool, United were out of that year's championship race. Sporting won the Cup Winners' Cup, West Ham the FA Cup and United finished the league season in second position, four points behind Liverpool.

It was a massive improvement in the side's fortunes to have gone so far in all three competitions. Having put together a young, settled side, Busby now made only the finest of adjustments to his team, tinkering with its components when necessary. He made two such signings in the spring of 1964. Goalkeeper Pat Dunne was bought from Shamrock Rovers for a fee of £10,500 and English international outside-right John Connelly came to Old Trafford from Burnley for a fee of £60,000.

There would be no further major signings for the next two and a half years because the club was diverting its financial resources into the erection of a new cantilevered north stand. The United directors had been informed in 1963 that Old Trafford had been chosen as one of the venues for the 1966 World Cup and they

March 1964 West Ham defeat United in the FA Cup semi-finals 3–1.

May 1964 The Manchester United youth team win the Youth Cup for the first time in seven years.

May 1964 United finish the league in second spot, four points behind champions Liverpool.

MANCHESTER UNITED **OFFICIAL MEMBERS' HISTORY BOOK** 61

were improving the ground's facilities for the tournament. The new construction would seat 10,500 spectators with a standing enclosure holding 10,000 more. It would also contain 34 heated executive boxes, an innovation for the UK, something that Busby had first seen on a visit to the USA. At a projected cost of £250,000 (it eventually cost £320,000) it sent United heavily into debt. Consequently, there was no money available to spend on strengthening the playing squad, but Busby had told his directors that in his opinion he would have little need of such funds in the near future.

It was easy to see where his confidence sprang from. United were now a seriously dynamic attacking force, with the flashing feet of Connelly on one wing and Best on the other. Law and Herd were rapier-sharp goalscorers while Crerand and Charlton complemented each other beautifully in the midfield. Brennan and Tony Dunne were established as the team's full-back partnership, Foulkes remained rock-solid at centre-half and Nobby Stiles would gradually become the first-choice half-back alongside him as the 1964/65 season progressed.

David Herd

Two defeats, three draws and one win in the opening six matches made for a less-than-impressive start to the season. Then five successive victories pushed off a run that eased United in among the championship contenders. The fifth, at the end of September 1964, came against Chelsea, one of their key rivals in the league and then managed by Tommy Docherty. United won 2–0 and played with such aplomb that they were sportingly cheered off the field at the end by the London crowd. "George scored a goal that night that I just stood and applauded," said Pat Crerand. "He changed feet so quickly and hit a screamer into the top corner. His performance was as good as Alfredo Di Stefano's for Real Madrid against Eintracht Frankfurt in the 1960 European Cup final, which was one of the great individual performances of all time."

Chelsea remained on top after that match, but United picked up nine points out of the 10 available to them in October 1964, culminating in a 7–0 victory over Aston Villa and a 2–0 win over champions Liverpool at Anfield that took the Old Trafford side a point clear of Docherty's team at the top of the table. It was a nice situation from which to launch another European expedition.

United's second place in the league at the end of the 1963/64 season provided the club with entry into the Fairs Cup, the precursor of the UEFA Cup. Their opening tie found them in a similar situation to that of the previous year, when they had met Willem II. This time they met the part-timers of IF Djurgardens in Stockholm in front of just 6,537 people. Again United stuttered to a 1–1 draw and again they trounced their part-time opponents in the Old Trafford return by 6–1.

The second round provided much tougher opposition: Borussia Dortmund of West Germany, who had been European Cup semi-finalists in the spring of 1964 and who were challenging for the Bundesliga title. United got off to a wonderful start at the Rote Erde Stadium when Herd and Charlton gave them a two-goal half-time lead. After the interval, Best went on one of his special runs, which ended with the ball in the back of the Dortmund net. The Germans pulled a goal back with a penalty and at that stage United were sitting on a superb away result. Nevertheless, in true United style, they went looking for more goals and a header from Law and a double from Charlton brought them a 6–1 victory.

The following midweek, four more United goals in the return with Dortmund at Old Trafford gave them a 10–2 aggregate in the tie. Things went less smoothly in the league.

TIMELINE

May 1964
Pat Dunne signs from Shamrock Rovers for £10,500 and John Connelly arrives from Burnley for £60,000.

June 1964
Old Trafford is selected as one of the host venues for the 1966 World Cup and work begins on the erection of a new cantilevered north stand.

October 1964
Denis Law hits four as United trounce Aston Villa 7–0.

During December and January an unlucky 1–0 home defeat by Leeds United and a series of drawn games pulled United back level with their chief pursuers, Chelsea and Leeds.

Everton were also going well in the league, but United's main business with them was in the Fairs Cup. Yet again, United had been drawn against an English side in Europe, and in the first leg at Old Trafford a close match ended 1–1.

The return at Goodison Park, watched by a crowd of 55,000, was equally tight but with United eventually victorious 2–1. The win sent them through to a quarter-final with Racing Strasbourg of France.

That return leg with Everton had been preceded by disappointing 1–0 defeats at Tottenham and Sunderland in the league, leaving United three points behind joint leaders Chelsea and Leeds as February ended. All three had 12 games left to play. It meant that Chelsea's visit to Old Trafford in mid-March 1965 would be crucial – United could not afford to lose if they were to maintain a serious title challenge.

The game began with one of the most extraordinary goals ever seen at the stadium. As Chelsea right-back Eddie McCreadie went to clear, Best raced at him, charging the ball down with his right leg after it had bounced between the two players. Best got his toe to it and sent it spinning towards the outside edge of the penalty area. Best's efforts left him off-balance and McCreadie got to the ball first but, under pressure from Best's constant movement at his back, unnerved by Best's audacity and persistence, and unsure where to turn, the Chelsea defender slipped and lost control of the ball. Best pounced on it and without pause dug under the ball with his right foot, scooping it high over the head of Chelsea goalkeeper Peter Bonetti, who had come to his near post, and into the far side of the goal. The tenacity, the speed of execution, the precision in this goal encapsulated Best's strengths. He was still only 18.

That goal knocked the stuffing out of

George Best, a football genius 'discovered' by United's Northern Ireland scout, Bob Bishop, in 1961.

Chelsea, who were overwhelmed by United's ceaseless attacking. With a double from Herd and one from Charlton, the match ended 4–0, putting United just one point behind Chelsea and Leeds. A fine, left-footed half-volley by Connelly gave United a 1–0 victory at Elland Road in mid-April, and two days later, on Easter Monday 1965, Manchester United were once more top of the First Division, with a 4–2 win at Birmingham City.

A 3–0 win over Liverpool followed and when United won their second-last match of the season, beating Arsenal 3–1 at Old Trafford, they were once again champions. As an attacking force, United were close to perfection. With both wingers extraordinarily sharp and quick, the ball was delivered into the box quickly, the midfielders were always pressing forward and Law's and Herd's swift reactions made goals more likely than not.

"We had a mixture of everything – guile, class, goalscorers and people who could mix it

October 1964
United defeat champions Liverpool 2–0.

November 1964
A hat-trick from Bobby Charlton helps United to a 6–1 victory over Borussia Dortmund in the Fairs Cup.

March 1965
Leeds beat United 1–0 in the FA Cup semi-final.

when required," said Denis Law of that team. "To have a championship side you really have got to have a mixture of all of those things."

That year, Louis Edwards succeeded Harold Hardman as chairman of the club on the latter's death. Edwards was friendly with Matt Busby and offered him strong support on the board of directors.

There was still much for United to play for over the remainder of the 1964/65 season. Although they had lost an FA Cup semi-final replay to Leeds in late March, they remained in the Fairs Cup. Bad weather had caused postponements and, together with FA Cup replays, had resulted in severe fixture congestion for United. As a result, the FA gave the club permission to extend their season. United therefore played their Fairs Cup tie with Strasbourg two weeks after their final league match. There were no hard and fast dates for European ties in those days, and it was up to the clubs to arrange dates for the fixtures.

A straightforward 5–0 win in the first leg in France on 12 May 1965 made the return a week later a formality. It was distinguished only by United receiving the league championship trophy and Law being presented with his trophy for European Footballer of the Year. A 0–0 draw put United into a semi-final with Hungarians Ferencvaros. With the rest of the First Division's footballers relaxing on the beach, United found themselves a goal down in the first leg at Old Trafford when Novak's long-distance free-kick streaked past Dunne. A penalty from Law evened it up and two goals from Herd put United into a 3–1 lead. A late goal from Rakosi made it 3–2.

The return, at the Nep Stadium in Budapest on 6 June, proved to be a physical battle, with the only goal coming from a penalty after the referee adjudged Stiles to have handled inside the penalty area. Novak netted from the spot. The away goals rule had yet to be introduced in

Nobby Stiles

European competition so the tie had to be decided by a replay. United lost the toss and had to return to Budapest 10 days later to try to win a place in the final with Juventus.

A 2–1 defeat ended United's campaign and Ferencvaros went on to beat Juventus 1–0 in the final.

The 1965/66 season saw United back in the European Cup, where they were untroubled by their first set of opponents, HJK Helsinki, winning 9–2 on aggregate. That was followed by home and away wins over ASK Vorwaerts Berlin, champions of East Germany, giving United another comfortable aggregate win – 5–1 this time. It took them into the quarter-finals, where they faced serious opposition in the shape of Lisbon side Benfica, the Portuguese champions.

One of the more notable aspects of the HJK Helsinki game was that George Best was dropped for the away leg. United had been out of sorts in the early stages of the season and Best had lost his place after Busby became concerned that the youngster's liking for nightlife was hindering his game.

By the time the first leg of the Benfica tie came round in February 1966, Best had been restored to the side but United's title hopes had been fading ever since a 2–1 defeat by Liverpool at Anfield on New Year's Day. There had been too much individuality and not enough teamwork on display in recent times, but everyone would have to pull together if Benfica, twice winners of the European Cup, in 1961 and 1962, and finalists in 1963 and 1965, were to be defeated.

United ended the first leg at Old Trafford 3–2 up to tee up a potentially tense return five weeks later at Benfica's Stadium of Light, where the Portuguese side had played 19 previous European Cup ties, winning 18 and drawing one. Busby, for one, would not be intimidated by that record or by Benfica's

TIMELINE

March 1985 United earn a crucial league victory over title rivals Chelsea courtesy of a superb individual effort from George Best and strikes from Charlton and Herd.

April 1985 Louis Edwards succeeds Harold Hardman as chairman of Manchester United following Hardman's death.

May 1985 After victories against Liverpool and Arsenal, United are crowned league champions.

80,000 home support. "It would be foolish to let Benfica get the initiative, especially here," he said. "We shall defend when necessary, and attack when we can, for to play defensively would be foolish for us. We shall play to the usual policy which won us the championship last year and we shall have four forwards just when we want them."

One of those forwards, Best, was just where United wanted him after six minutes when Tony Dunne angled a free-kick into the Benfica penalty area. A deft flick of the head from the United winger produced the opening goal. Best excelled further when he took a Herd knockdown in his stride and went whirring past three defenders at speed before clipping the ball past goalkeeper Costa Pereira to make it 2–0. When Connelly made it 3–0 to United there were only 15 minutes on the clock. An own goal from Shay Brennan in the second half gave Benfica a glimmer of hope, but strikes from Crerand and Charlton meant the game ended 5–1 in United's favour. It was one of the greatest of all European Cup performances and it delighted Matt Busby. He stated afterwards that he thought it had been United's finest hour.

"As to whether we play it off the cuff, well we always hold tactical talks every week and before every match," he said. "But we do encourage individualism, especially that of Best, Charlton and Law. Because unless you encourage that sort of individualism, you really have nothing."

The semi-final brought back memories for several of the United party – it took place at the Yugoslav People's Army Stadium, Belgrade, where the Busby Babes had played their last match before the Munich crash. This time United's opponents were not Red Star but Belgrade's other major club, Partizan. The Yugoslavs made it clear beforehand that they felt they needed a clear two-goal lead to take to Old Trafford for the second leg. They got the first of those goals shortly after half-time when Hasanagic headed past Gregg and they got the second when Becejac controlled the ball in style before spinning to shoot past the United goalkeeper.

Even worse, Best seriously aggravated a knee injury he had been carrying. His season was over and he would need a cartilage operation.

Busby remained confident for the second leg, but Partizan defended in depth and United badly missed Best's ingenuity in their attempts at breaking down the Yugoslavs' defence. With just over quarter of an hour remaining, Nobby Stiles finally found a weak spot in the Partizan resistance and threaded a shot past goalkeeper Milutin Soskic, but it was too late. Partizan held on for a place in the final with Real Madrid in Brussels.

United ended the season fourth in the First Division, 10 points behind champions Liverpool. Once again they crashed out of the FA Cup at the semi-final stage, losing 1–0 to Everton just three days after the second leg with Partizan. Losing the European Cup semi was the most bitter blow, though, and several of United's senior players wondered whether they would ever again get such a good opportunity to lift the trophy.

The only way back into Europe's premier competition was by winning the league and in 1966/67 United directed almost all of their efforts to that end. A surprise fourth-round exit from the FA Cup at home to Second Division Norwich City, and defeat by Blackpool in their only League Cup tie that season would allow plenty of recovery time in between league fixtures. The line-up remained settled and for the opening match with West Brom at Old Trafford on 20 August 1966. Best

returned to the right wing, with Connelly switching to the left.

In the opening minute of that game, Charlton, a World Cup winner with England three weeks previously, passed the ball into the path of Best, who opened United's goals account for the season. By the 20th minute, the score was 5–1 to United and the points were in the bag. United had started as they meant to continue, slackening off to allow West Brom a couple of goals for a final score of 5–3. In the early weeks of that 1966/67 season, Best and Law were in fine individual form and United played some stunning football, but there were also some careless defeats and the defence looked shaky at times.

Busby realized some adjustments were needed. In September 1966, he made what turned out to be a far-reaching change, signing Alex Stepney from Chelsea for £55,000, a record fee for a goalkeeper. Stepney immediately made the goalkeeping position his own. Connelly, 28, was replaced by the younger John Aston and moved on to Blackburn Rovers for £40,000. David Sadler,

Bobby Charlton shows off the league championship trophy in May 1967.

TIMELINE

April 1966	April 1966	May 1966
Partizan Belgrade defeat United 2–1 on aggregate in the European Cup semi-final.	Everton defeat United 1–0 in the FA Cup semi-final.	United finish the season in fourth place.

still only 23, became a regular over the season, sometimes at centre-half, sometimes in midfield, sometimes at centre-forward.

Shay Brennan and Bill Foulkes were both dropped after a particularly poor performance led to defeat at Blackpool in October. Foulkes had made more than 500 appearances for the club – only the second player to do so after Joe Spence – and was 34 years old, but he was soon restored to the team. Tony Dunne was switched to right-back in place of Brennan with Bobby Noble, a 20-year-old, coming into the side in the other full-back position.

Chelsea, still under the management of Tommy Docherty, were once again setting the pace at the top of the league. United went to Stamford Bridge at the start of November and, with Best in inspirational form, came away 3–1 winners. By the end of that month United were top of the First Division. They lost just one more league game – away to Sheffield United on Boxing Day – between then and the end of the season. United and Liverpool took turns at topping the table in the opening three months of 1967, but by April United were two points clear although the slightest slip would spell disaster as they were being pursued by no fewer than five clubs.

As their rivals stumbled, United coped with the pressure and on 6 May 1967 they travelled to Upton Park to face West Ham United in their penultimate fixture of the season, knowing a point would give them the title. With a post-war record crowd of 38,424 inside the ground, United settled the issue in style. Goals from Charlton, Crerand and Foulkes put them 3–0 ahead after just 10 minutes. Best and Law added to the tally after the interval, and with 10 minutes remaining Law hit a sixth to give United a 6–1 victory.

United finished as champions once again, four points clear of nearest challengers

John Aston

Nottingham Forest. There was champagne in the dressing-room and the following day Matt Busby gave his thoughts on the triumph.

"I don't think we would have won the championship without Stepney. The cup defeat at Norwich, although a bitter disappointment at the time, proved to be a good thing. With only the league to worry about we have been better equipped both physically and mentally. Ability is no longer enough – although there is no substitute for it. You have to have a combination of ability plus work rate. We would obviously like to win the championship again. But we all feel that we must have a real go at winning the European Cup."

The 1967/68 campaign began well. A straightforward 4–0 aggregate win over minnows Hibernians of Malta in the first round of the European Cup gave United a second-round tie against FC Sarajevo of Yugoslavia. The first leg was scheduled for mid-November and United travelled to Eastern Europe as league leaders after a 2–1 victory over Liverpool the previous Saturday. Sarajevo proved physically tough, dishing out severe physical punishment to United forwards Best, Charlton and homegrown 18-year-old Brian Kidd, but at the end of the 90 minutes United had a 0–0 draw to show for their pains.

There was more of the same to come from Sarajevo in Manchester, but they were finally brought to heel when Fahrudin Prijaca was sent off for an ugly, slicing tackle on Best. By then, United were a goal up through John Aston and they capitalized on their one-man advantage when Best made it 2–0 midway through the second half. Two goals down, the Yugoslavs started to play some neat football and got a goal back, but United, backed by a 62,000 crowd, hung on for the win.

The quarter-finals, where they met Polish champions Gornik Zabrze, proved equally tough. Best was again subjected to a series of

June 1966
Bobby Charlton, Nobby Stiles and John Connelly play for England in the World Cup triumph.

September 1966
Alex Stepney joins United from Chelsea for a record £55,000 fee. John Connelly (right) is sold to Blackburn for £40,000

March 1967
David Herd breaks his leg scoring against Leicester City, marking the end of his United career.

MANCHESTER UNITED **OFFICIAL MEMBERS' HISTORY BOOK**   67

fouls in the first leg, at Old Trafford, but he maintained his discipline and in the second half his low, hard centre forced Gornik centre-half Florenski to stretch for the ball and put through his own goal. A last-minute, close-range effort from Kidd made the scoreline much more comfortable for United. On a snow-covered pitch in Katowice for the return, in a game watched by 100,000 Poles, United looked surefooted in the tricky conditions. Snow fell steadily during the game and soon it was impossible to see the pitch markings, but Italian referee Concetto Lo Bello let the match continue. A second-half strike from Wlodek Lubanski had United living on their nerves, but they held out for the aggregate 2–1 win.

"It was too much of a gamble," said Busby afterwards. "It would have been a sad way to have gone out. This is a prize we have been fighting for for years and it would have been terrible if a two-goal lead had been lost under conditions such as they were."

United were three points clear of Liverpool at the top of the league on Boxing Day 1967 and they retained that three-point lead for the

succeeding two months. Three calamitous defeats in March – by Chelsea, Coventry City and Manchester City – pulled them back within reach of the chasing pack but by late April they were top once again as they prepared for their European Cup semi-final against Real Madrid. The Spanish champions and six-times European Cup winners held no fears for Busby. "I feel this is our year," he said. "I think things are running for us this time and I feel happier than on previous occasions when we have got so far. We were the first English club to enter the European Cup because we felt it was a world game. It is the one thing the club wants to win and the one thing I want to win."

The first leg was played at Old Trafford and although United struggled to find fluency a goal from Best decided the game.

Three days later, away to West Bromwich Albion in the league, United went down 6–3, leaving their title hopes hanging by a thread. That defeat allowed Manchester City to go top of the First Division for the first time that season. United won their next match, against Newcastle United 6–0, but in their final league

Manchester United, 1968 European champions

May 1967
A 6–1 victory against West Ham secures the championship for United.

August 1967
Brian Kidd makes his United debut, aged 18.

May 1968
A 2–1 defeat to Sunderland means United finish second in the league, two points behind champions Manchester City.

outing of the season they trooped off the pitch after a 2–1 home defeat by Sunderland. It handed the title to City. United were second on 56 points, two behind their local rivals.

It didn't seem like the best send-off for the trip to Real's multi-tiered Bernabeu Stadium. And by the interval a bewildered United were 3–1 behind to a dazzling display from the hosts. There was silence in the United dressing-room at half-time, with the players traumatized at having been pulled apart by Real. Busby quietly reminded them that they were only a goal behind on aggregate and that one goal would get them back on level terms.

The United players gradually grew in confidence. With 15 minutes to go, Best's header found Sadler, in for the injured Law, and he clipped the ball past Betancourt in the Real goal. Five minutes on, Bill Foulkes pounded forward, gathered a pass from Best and planted the ball in the Real net to make the final aggregate score 4–3 to United. It was a suitably glorious, and dramatic, way for United to make history, paving the way for Matt Busby to crown his career by lifting the greatest trophy in club football.

Bobby Charlton thought that it was fated that United would win the 1968 European Cup after the dramatic semi-final with Real Madrid. United had a more tangible advantage for the final in that the match was to be played at Wembley, but they were without Denis Law, who watched from his hospital bed after a cartilage operation. The sides' first-choice strips were identical so United wore all-blue, Benfica all-white.

It was a fractious match, with tight marking and tackling, and it boiled over into a brawl just before the interval. The teams left the field at half-time to the booing of the crowd after a tense first half.

Eight minutes after the break, Sadler curved a clever cross into the penalty area, where Charlton glanced a neat header past Henrique. But with nine minutes remaining, Benfica struck back through Jaime Graca.

Eusebio had chances to wrap it up for

29 May 1968: David Sadler holds the European Cup aloft on a night that saw all Matt Busby's dreams fulfilled.

Benfica in the final five minutes but the match headed into extra-time.

After three minutes, a long kick from Stepney was flicked on by Kidd to Best who whisked the ball away from his marker, deftly sent Henrique the wrong way, sidestepped him in style and sidefooted the ball into the unguarded goal.

The crowd barely had time to get used to United being in the lead again when Sadler headed Charlton's corner goalwards. Kidd headed it on, Henrique saved and Kidd, on his 19th birthday, rose to the rebound, sending a second header arcing over Henrique's outstretched fingers and into the net.

Minutes later, Kidd raced up the right wing and crossed low and hard for Charlton to send a magnificent scooped shot spinning over Henrique and into the net. Eusebio had two good, hard shots saved well by Stepney in the second half of extra-time, but United stayed in control, finishing 4–1 winners.

"That was my greatest moment," said Matt Busby. "I had lived for it for a long time. This was the combination of all my ideas, my ambitions – winning the European Cup."

May 1968
Manchester United win the European Cup…

May 1968
… Matt Busby is knighted for services to football…

May 1968
… and George Best is named European Footballer of the Year.

MANCHESTER UNITED **OFFICIAL MEMBERS' HISTORY BOOK**   69

Even though Matt Busby moved 'upstairs' from the manager's office, he remained a powerful influence on club affairs.

CHAPTER EIGHT

THE END OF AN ERA

Within a year of winning the European Cup, Matt Busby brought his managerial career to a close. But Busby's shadow loomed large as successive managers tried in vain to emulate his huge achievements...

The successor to Matt Busby was always going to be presented with a difficult task. Wilf McGuinness and then Frank O'Farrell tried their best to fill his shoes but both had limited success, and the post-Busby years soon found United on a dangerous downward spiral.

Matt Busby's passionate desire to win the European Cup had been driven by his belief that increased international club competition would improve the British game. Sadly, that belief was strained to the limit early in the 1968/69 season. By beating Benfica, United gained entry to the World Club Cup, a two-leg prestige match between the European and South American champions. United's opponents in the autumn of 1968 were Estudiantes de La Plata of Argentina.

There were serious overtones even before the match began. Nobby Stiles and Bobby Charlton had been members of the England team that had beaten Argentina in the World Cup quarter-final two years previously, after which England manager Alf Ramsey implied that the Argentinians had acted like "animals". Then, in 1967, six players had been sent off in a violent World Club Cup play-off between Celtic and Racing Club of Argentina.

"It is so difficult for any manager to ensure there is no hot-headedness and that players do not retaliate," said Busby before the first leg in Buenos Aires on 25 September 1968. "You can do all the talking in the world and advise in every way, but somebody on the field will be provoked and do something they really do not want to do. But this is a world game and we must try to break down barriers."

There were 2,000 police keeping an eye on the 85,000 crowd. That ensured there were no problems off the field but on it the Argentinians ceaselessly punched and spat on the United players, goading them with numerous on- and off-the-ball fouls. The two World Cup men were particularly badly treated – Stiles required stitches in an eye injury and Charlton's leg was sliced open. Late in the match, Stiles was dismissed for disputing a dubious decision by the Uruguayan linesman. Estudiantes' Conigliaro had headed the only goal of the game in the 29th minute.

In the return leg at Old Trafford three weeks later, Denis Law left the field after Estudiantes' goalkeeper Poletti's studs had become embedded in the United forward's leg. That was after Veron had headed Estudiantes 1–0 ahead. Late in the match, George Best was sent off with Estudiantes' centre-back Hugo Medina after a punch-up. Medina had to be held back by a linesman as the Argentinian attempted to thump Best on their way to the dressing-rooms. Willie Morgan, a winger whom Busby had signed from Burnley for £100,000 in the summer, equalized but Estudiantes took the World Club Cup, now a tarnished trophy, with a 2–1 aggregate.

United's defence of the European Cup was more enjoyable. After a 10–2 aggregate victory over Irish champions Waterford, they faced Anderlecht. A 3–0 win at Old Trafford set them up nicely for the return in Brussels,

TIMELINE

October 1968
South American champions Estudiantes beat United 2–1 on aggregate in an ill-tempered World Club Cup match.

January 1969
On 14 January 1969, Matt Busby announces that he will be resigning at the end of the season.

April 1969
The European Cup semi-final first-leg match against AC Milan is beamed back live to 25,000 fans watching on a big screen at Old Trafford. Milan win 2–0.

MANCHESTER UNITED **OFFICIAL MEMBERS' HISTORY BOOK** 71

Brian Kidd causes havoc in the six-yard box during United's 1968/69 European Cup semi-final against AC Milan, but the Italian side would triumph 2–1 on aggregate.

where newly introduced midfielder Carlo Sartori gave United a 1–0 lead. Anderlecht threw everything into attack and fought back to lead 3–1. They were just unable to get a fourth. The United players applauded a distinguished set of opponents off the pitch. That aggregate win put United into a quarter-final with Rapid Vienna.

On 14 January 1969, Matt Busby announced that he would be resigning at the end of the season. He was almost 60 and had been manager for nearly a quarter of a century.

"It is only right that my successor should be ready to start at the beginning of a new season," said Busby.

Rapid Vienna were overwhelmed by United in the first leg at Old Trafford in March. Two goals from Best and one from Morgan produced a superb 3–0 victory. For his second, Best exchanged passes with Stiles before dancing across the face of the Rapid defence, evading a series of barbed tackles. Then, while falling backwards and with four men still between him and the goal, he spiked the ball

into the roof of the Rapid net. A goalless draw in Austria a week later sent United into the semi-finals.

Winter postponements meant that United had a backlog of fixtures and they were given special dispensation by the Football Association to extend their season into mid-May for their European Cup semi-final with AC Milan. The first leg, in the San Siro, was watched by 85,000 people inside the stadium and by 200 million on television across Europe. The match was beamed back to Old Trafford, where nearly 25,000 fans watched it on big screens at the ground.

Milan dominated from the start. In the 34th minute, Foulkes failed to head clear convincingly and Crerand mistimed his attempt at booting the ball away. It rebounded off his back and Angelo Sormani swooped to plant it past Jimmy Rimmer in the United goal. Sormani missed an open goal shortly after the break but with 50 minutes gone, Kurt Hamrin ended an excellent Milan move by steering home the Italians' second. The night became

TIMELINE

May 1969
Bobby Charlton scores in the European Cup semi-final second leg, but United are beaten 2–1 on aggregate by AC Milan.

May 1969
A 3–2 home win over Leicester City on 17 May marks the end of Matt Busby's brilliant managerial career. Or does it…?

June 1969
Wilf McGuinness is promoted from reserve team coach to become the new 'chief coach' of Manchester United.

72   MANCHESTER UNITED OFFICIAL MEMBERS' HISTORY BOOK

even more bleak when John Fitzpatrick was dismissed for kicking Hamrin in an off-the-ball incident.

"We are not beaten yet," said Busby after the 2–0 defeat. "We never give up when we have a chance. If we can score one at Old Trafford that will worry them and a second will earn us a replay."

On the night of the second leg, the Italians were forced to defend in depth as United swarmed towards their goal, but intensive defending was something Italian sides delighted in. Rimmer did make a crucial save from midfielder Gianni Rivera but Milan goalkeeper Fabio Cudicini made many more. It took until the 70th minute for United to open the scoring. Best steered clear of three of the Italian defenders who had shackled him all evening and found Charlton, who swiftly hit the target with a fine, angled shot. United now redoubled their efforts in search of an equalizer. Ten minutes on, Crerand sent a low ball into the Milan six-yard box and Law appeared to have shepherded it over the line before it was hacked away. United players who were on the spot were convinced it was a goal but French referee Machin waved play on.

"My team were magnificent and gave everything they had to pull the game around," commented Busby afterwards. United had succumbed showing the spirit that had always marked Matt Busby's teams. Two days later, the Boss drew down the curtain on his managerial career, waving farewell to the fans at the final league game of the season, a 3–2 win over Leicester City.

A new structure at Old Trafford was designed to ease the burden of living up to Busby's reputation. On 1 June 1969, Wilf McGuinness stepped up from the position of reserve team coach to become chief coach. Busby, as general manager, was to work with

Wilf McGuinness (left), Matt Busby's immediate successor.

McGuinness to relieve some of the pressure on him. McGuinness was responsible for team selection, tactics, training and the coaching of the senior side. Busby would oversee all the other aspects of the manager's job, such as dealing with press enquiries, players' wages and transfer business. It freed McGuinness, still only 31 years old, to work purely as a coach. Due to injury ending his career prematurely, McGuinness had already been an England youth coach and a coach to the national team's 1966 World Cup-winning squad.

"We'll just see how it works out," said Busby. "We've been watching Wilf closely as he has gone about his duties and we're satisfied he can do the job. Perhaps he lacks experience but he knows our ways and he has plenty to bite on for the moment. In a year or so, perhaps he could have full command."

McGuinness did indeed have much to chew over as he prepared for pre-season training. United had raised their game for the 1968/69 European Cup, but had finished 11th in the First Division, their lowest position for six years, and had been knocked out in the FA Cup quarter-finals. His first game was away to Crystal Palace, where United treated the biggest crowd of the day – 48,000 – to a fine show of clever, passing football on a sweltering August afternoon. With Best, Morgan, Kidd and Law up front, prompted by Crerand and Charlton in midfield, United attacked from all directions. Only John Jackson in the Palace goal prevented United from hitting the Londoners for six and the match ended 2–2.

Disappointingly, this was followed by a 2–0 home defeat by Everton and things got worse the following Saturday when United were beaten 4–1 at home by Southampton. Bill Foulkes had struggled to cope with probing crosses and Ron Davies took full advantage to notch all four of the Saints' goals.

December 1969
Manchester City beat United 4–3 on aggregate in the League Cup semi-finals.

January 1970
United exact revenge for their League Cup derby defeat, beating Manchester City 3–0 in the FA Cup fourth round.

March 1970
The Reds suffer another semi-final loss, this time losing an FA Cup replay 1–0 to Leeds United (the first match had ended 0–0).

MANCHESTER UNITED **OFFICIAL MEMBERS' HISTORY BOOK**   **73**

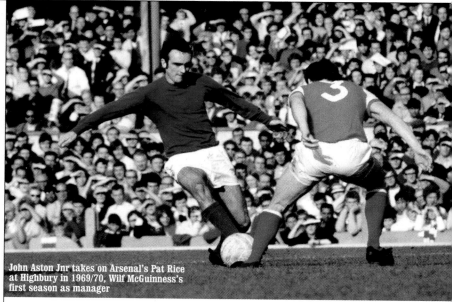

John Aston Jnr takes on Arsenal's Pat Rice
at Highbury in 1969/70, Wilf McGuinness's
first season as manager

"Uneasiness at the back," was Busby's terse explanation of how United had lost the game. He suggested to McGuinness that Arsenal centre-half Ian Ure would make a good replacement for Foulkes and within hours Ure was at Old Trafford, purchased for £80,000.

Ure, a Scottish international, was best known to the United support as the man who had fought a running battle with Denis Law in a league game two years previously, as a result of which both men were given six-week suspensions. A strong stopper, Ure brought stability to the team through his central defensive partnership with David Sadler. His arrival ended Foulkes's distinguished playing career. United's results gradually began to improve. They finished the 1969/70 league season in eighth position.

The two domestic cup competitions yielded fair results. A lengthy League Cup run produced a semi-final with Manchester City. In the first leg, at Maine Road on 3 December 1969, the score was 1–1 when, two minutes from time, City's Francis Lee tumbled over Ure's leg and City were given a penalty, much to the chagrin of the United players. City scored but even then it took an outstanding save from goalkeeper Joe Corrigan and a goal-line clearance from Tony Book to preserve their lead. At the end of the match, Best was seen to jostle the referee, knocking the ball out of the official's hands. He was later fined £100 and suspended for four weeks for that incident.

A crisp atmosphere surrounded the Old Trafford return a fortnight later when goals from young defender Paul Edwards and Law put United 2–1 up and level on aggregate. With seven minutes remaining, Lee hit an indirect free-kick at goal. Stepney had no need to make any attempt to save but he parried the ball instinctively and Mike Summerbee pounced, putting the ball in the net and City in the final.

A month later, United exacted revenge with a 3–0 home win over City in the FA Cup, part of a run that took them to the semi-finals. There they met Leeds United and after two 0–0 draws, lost the second replay 1–0. On the afternoon of the first replay, McGuinness had found Best ignoring team orders by absenting himself in a girl's bedroom. Late in the match,

April 1970
United finish the 1969/70 season in eighth place in the league table, having won 14, drawn 17 and lost 11 matches out of 42.

December 1970
United reach their third semi-final under Wilf McGuinness, but are eliminated from the League Cup 3–2 (agg) by Aston Villa.

December 1970
On 29 December, Wilf McGuinness is demoted to trainer-coach of the reserves. Matt Busby returns as caretaker manager.

the Irishman had a fine scoring opportunity that could have decided the tie but he stumbled over the ball. Leeds went on to lose the final, beaten by Chelsea in a replay at Old Trafford. A run of bad results at the start of the 1970/71 season left United sixth from bottom at the end of August. The team looked spiritless and rumbles of discontent about McGuinness were getting back to Busby.

As goalkeeper Alex Stepney later opined: "Wilf wasn't very good at handling players at training. It wasn't all his fault perhaps, but he lacked experience."

The team's form picked up very slightly during the autumn and gave McGuinness some encouragement. However, a hard-fought, sometimes vicious, local derby with City at Old Trafford in December resulted in a 4–1 defeat. Arsenal, second in the table, were next at Old Trafford in the league and United were played off the park, beaten 3–1 in front of the lowest home crowd of the season – 33,182. On the two Wednesdays either side of that game, United played their two-leg League Cup semi-final against Aston Villa of the Third Division. Villa were the best team in each leg, completing a 3–2 aggregate victory in front of their fans that had the Birmingham crowd chanting "Easy, Easy" at the end.

Willie Morgan

Now in serious danger of relegation, United's 4–4 draw at Derby County on Boxing Day proved to be the last throw of the dice for McGuinness. On 29 December 1970, Busby stated, "The directors called a special meeting last night to discuss the performance of the team and decided to relieve Mr McGuinness of his duties as team manager. As he did not want to leave the club and as the club felt he still had a part to play, he has been offered his former position as trainer-coach to the Central League team, which he has accepted. I am sorry it has not worked out because Wilf McGuinness was my choice."

"Obviously, it's disappointing to me, but managers are judged by results," rationalised McGuinness at the time. "With a bit of luck we might have been in three cup finals, but it wasn't to be."

In later years, McGuinness would reflect that with the benefit of hindsight, he would have stood more chance of succeeding if Matt Busby had stayed on as manager initially and he had come in as his number two to learn the ropes.

Instead, following McGuinness's demotion, Busby reluctantly took over as caretaker manager – "I thought I had left all this behind me," he said.

Stability was injected into the United side and they had manoeuvred themselves into eighth position by the end of the season. Busby bowed out in style at Maine Road on 5 May. City enlisted *This Is Your Life* presenter Eamonn Andrews to make a special presentation to the great man and his team presented him with 90 minutes of graceful, flowing football as they defeated their old rivals 4–3 with Law, Best and Charlton, appropriately, scoring all four United goals.

On 8 June 1971, Busby's second successor was announced – Frank O'Farrell. He was appointed team manager while Busby was to join the board of directors.

As a half-back, Cork-born O'Farrell had played for West Ham United and Preston North End in the 1950s. He went on to manage Weymouth with whom he won the Southern League championship twice in five years. In 1968, after three years at Torquay United during which time they were promoted, he joined Leicester City. City had just won promotion back to the First Division when O'Farrell, then in his early Forties, joined United.

O'Farrell said, "I shall have full control at Old Trafford. I have been given that assurance. Sir Matt Busby will be on the board, but I shall be the manager in every sense of the word."

May 1971
United finish eighth in the league and Matt Busby bows out with a final day 4–3 win over Manchester City.

June 1971
On 8 June 1971, Frank O'Farrell is named as the new Manchester United manager.

August 1971
George Best sits down on the pitch after being sent off during United's 3–2 win against Chelsea at Stamford Bridge.

Busby was delighted with the new man in charge. "I look upon Frank O'Farrell as my last great signing, possibly the greatest of the lot," he gushed.

As well as a new manager, there would be a new backdrop to the action at Old Trafford. Building work, which would last a year, began in 1971 to extend the cantilever stand round behind the goal at the traditional Scoreboard End. The scoreboard itself was to be replaced by an electronic screen which would give scores, news and announcements.

Thunder and lightning heralded the start of United's league season, which began at Derby County, the scene of McGuinness's final outing as United manager. A 2–0 half-time lead was surrendered early in the second half and only a string of superb saves by Alex Stepney stopped Derby snatching a winner. There were more dramatics the following Wednesday at Stamford Bridge when George Best sat down on the pitch after being dismissed by referee Norman Burtenshaw. United recorded a useful 3–2 victory.

Hooliganism had plagued United for several years. The Fairs Cup semi-final with Ferencvaros back in 1965 had been held up after missiles were thrown onto the pitch from the Stretford End. The same thing had happened during the 1969 European Cup semi-final when Milan goalkeeper Cudicini was felled by an object thrown from the crowd. In the spring of 1971, during a 2–0 home defeat by Newcastle, a knife was thrown onto the pitch, prompting an FA Disciplinary Committee to punish United by ordering the club to play their opening two home fixtures of the 1971/72 season at least 25 miles from Old Trafford. That first "home" match, at Anfield, drew a crowd of just 27,649 for the meeting with champions Arsenal. Best was in effervescent form and Kidd was thriving under O'Farrell and they helped United to come from a goal down to win 3–1.

Frank O'Farrell

For the final goal, Kidd swerved round three defenders before sending a shot flashing past Bob Wilson.

Only 23,000 were at United's next "home" match, this time at the Victoria Ground, Stoke. Best sashayed and swayed past opponents in brilliant fashion time and again throughout the 90 minutes. He scored twice and inspired United to a 3–1 win over West Bromwich Albion that put them briefly on top of the First Division. After his sending-off against Chelsea, Best, who was already sitting on a six-week suspension, seemed in real danger of a three-month ban but this did not seem to faze him one bit. As it turned out, his explanation of the Chelsea incident – that he had been swearing at team-mate Willie Morgan and not the referee – was accepted and he incurred no further punishment for the incident.

A golden autumn yielded an exceptional run of results and as Christmas approached, United were top of the First Division and five points clear of nearest challengers Derby and Manchester City. That lead was whittled away game by game as United faltered to a series of disappointing draws over the Christmas period. The new year began with Best missing training for the week before United lost 3–1 at home to Wolverhampton Wanderers. He was fined two weeks' wages and ordered to move out of his high-tech, futuristic new home in Bramhall and back into digs with his original landlady, Mrs Fullaway, in Chorlton.

It did little to help United deal with their alarming decline. Best was off-form on his return and they tumbled from the top in late January, dropping down to third after a 1–0 home defeat by Chelsea. With the defence looking flimsy and the attack lacking fizz, United were soon in freefall. After a 5–1 hammering at Leeds they were in seventh position. By mid-March, they had gone 11 league games without a win, prompting

George Best's popularity with the fans never waned, but Frank O'Farrell put the wayward Irish genius on the transfer list after he missed training three times in one week in December 1972.

O'Farrell to start spending on new signings. The first was Martin Buchan, a stylish centre-back who cost £125,000 from Aberdeen. Ian Storey-Moore, a graceful goalscoring winger, cost £200,000 from Nottingham Forest. Buchan strengthened the defence and Storey-Moore pepped up the attack. United were steadied and finished the 1971/72 season in eighth place.

It proved to be a temporary reprieve. By December 1972, United, table-toppers at exactly the same stage the previous year, were sixth from last, just two points above bottom club Crystal Palace. Ted MacDougall had been bought from Bournemouth for £200,000 and Wyn Davies from Manchester City for £25,000 in the autumn, but both strikers failed to spark the United attack. More worrying was the lack of respect and loyalty O'Farrell managed to inspire in his players, many of whom still addressed Busby as "Boss" in his presence.

George Best was the rock on which O'Farrell finally foundered. While the team struggled on the pitch, Best was struggling to turn up for training. Matters came to a head at the start of December 1972 when he was dropped after having failed to appear three times in a week. At a board meeting on 5 December, he was placed on the transfer list and suspended for 14 days. But on 14 December, without O'Farrell's knowledge, Busby and Louis Edwards privately agreed with Best to lift his punishment. Despite his authority having been so blatantly undermined, O'Farrell refused to resign. If Busby and Edwards no longer had confidence in him, they would have to sack him.

Minus Best, United travelled to London to face Crystal Palace on 16 December 1972 and in the opening minute, Jackson saved superbly from Storey-Moore. Then the walls caved in as Palace strolled to an easy 5–0 win. United were now second from bottom and staring relegation in the face. Three days later, O'Farrell was gone from Old Trafford.

After more than three years, United were still searching for Busby's successor.

March 1972
Frank O'Farrell splashes out £125,000 to buy centre-back Martin Buchan and £200,000 on winger Ian Storey-Moore.

April 1972
United finish in eighth position in the league for the third consecutive season.

December 1972
Three days after a disastrous 5–0 defeat at Crystal Palace, Frank O'Farrell is sacked.

The pugnacious
Tommy Docherty wanted
to be the best manager
in the world.

CHAPTER NINE
GOING DOWN RISING UP

Under Tommy Docherty, Manchester United were relegated to play Second Division football for the first time in 37 years. But 'The Doc' eventually managed to rekindle flair and success at Old Trafford...

ommy Docherty had been a spectator at Selhurst Park for the first half of United's catastrophic defeat by Crystal Palace in December 1972. He watched the second half as manager-elect of the Old Trafford club. In the boardroom at half-time, he had been asked if he would like to take over at United. Docherty, then the manager of the Scottish national team, immediately said 'yes'.

Frank O'Farrell was sacked the following Tuesday, and Docherty was officially installed that Friday, 22 December 1972.

A fine footballer, Docherty had spent most of his playing career at Preston North End. He helped them reach the 1954 FA Cup final playing alongside winger Tom Finney who tipped Docherty to be a great manager one day. Docherty was aiming higher – he wanted to be the best manager in the world.

He began his managerial career at Chelsea in 1962. After five years during which time he won the League Cup, he bossed Rotherham United, Queen's Park Rangers, Aston Villa, and Porto before some fine work for Scotland earned him a call from Old Trafford

"I have always thought this was the greatest club in the world," he said on his arrival.

Docherty immediately imposed his own identity on the club. George Graham had conveniently been placed on the Arsenal transfer list on the day O'Farrell was sacked, and five days after Docherty's appointment he splashed out £120,000 for the Scottish international midfielder. The following day,

another of Docherty's Scottish internationals, Under-23 full-back Alex Forsyth, was signed for £100,000 from Partick Thistle.

Pat Crerand was promoted from youth coach to assistant manager. "He is a man I can trust and that's important," said Docherty.

As 1973 began, Docherty purchased Jim Holton, another Scot and a hugely aggressive centre-half, from Shrewsbury Town for £80,000. Lou Macari, a striker, arrived from Celtic for £200,000 in mid-January, bringing Docherty's total spending in less than a month to the awe-inspiring sum of £450,000.

The fee for 23-year-old Macari was a record for a player moving from Scotland to England. At Celtic Park, the Scot of Italian descent scored 57 goals in 102 games and at the time of his transfer had already won two Scottish League titles and two Scottish Cup medals. He had also begun an international career that would yield 24 caps and an appearance at the 1978 World Cup finals.

There were eight Scots in the side that drew with West Ham United at Old Trafford in late January 1973 – Forsyth, Denis Law, Holton, Martin Buchan, Willie Morgan, Ted MacDougall, Macari and Graham. That game produced United's first league point of the year. United were 2–0 down but a Bobby Charlton penalty and a close-range shot by debutant Macari levelled the score.

Docherty's team were uncompromising and aggressive in their pursuit of points. Graham was used as a holding player in a pragmatic 4–4–2 formation that was more defensively

TIMELINE

December 1972
On 22 December 1972, Tommy Docherty is appointed manager of Manchester United.

December 1972
Days after his appointment, Docherty buys George Graham for £120,000 from Arsenal, and Alex Forsyth for £100,000 from Partick Thistle.

January 1973
The Doc's spending spree continues as he buys big centre-half Jim Holton (right) from Shrewsbury Town for £80,000 and striker Lou Macari from Celtic for £200,000.

oriented than anything United fans had seen before. And Docherty would frequently use the long-ball game, skipping the midfield to seek out his strikers.

It wasn't pretty and pretty often it was ineffective – it took nearly two months for him to record his first victory as United manager. Eventually, though, United scrambled out of the relegation mire. Macari and Brian Kidd were Docherty's preferred strikeforce so Ted MacDougall had been offloaded to West Ham in February 1973 for £150,000.

Bobby Charlton reached a notable landmark when he made his 600th league appearance, against Stoke City in April 1973. Two days after that game, Charlton announced that he would be retiring at the end of the season.

"I would have hated to leave under worse circumstances but things are rosier now," he said. "I am delighted to see Tommy Docherty doing so well."

He bade farewell to 58,000 Old Trafford fans on Easter Monday against Sheffield United. The following Saturday a chant of "Sir Bobby Charlton" bounced around Stamford Bridge as he made his final appearance against Chelsea, and then one of the greatest of all United players was gone.

As one legend left, another returned. George Best, who had been absent from Old Trafford for five months, was given training facilities at the club. Denis Law, the other member of United's great 1960s treble act, was given a free transfer by Docherty two days after Charlton's swansong against Chelsea. Law had played in the first team just three times since Docherty's arrival. Another long-time United servant, David Sadler, went to Preston North End on a free transfer that summer.

Off the field, a consortium of businessmen mounted a takeover bid. They wanted the United board to resign and wished to reinstate Frank O'Farrell in place of Docherty. The board responded with an Extraordinary General Meeting in mid-April 1973 at which it was agreed that first option on any sale of shares should be given to the existing directors. This further increased Louis

The legendary Bobby Charlton waves goodbye at Stamford Bridge, his final appearance in the United shirt.

TIMELINE

February 1973	April 1973	July 1973
On 10 February, United record their first victory under Docherty, a 2–1 home win over Wolves.	Bobby Charlton plays his final game for United at Stamford Bridge on the last day of the season.	Another United legend, Denis Law, joins Manchester City on a free transfer.

Edwards' power at Old Trafford.

The new season promised a fresh start, but four defeats in the first six games left United seventh from bottom. The team lacked inspiration but Best was back again, looking to regain his place in the team. Docherty expressed himself "delighted" at Best's return. Best said: "I've missed the game more than I thought I would. I would like to think that the drinking problems I had, and the depressions they caused, are behind me."

Joe Lancaster, a specialist fitness coach, was brought in to help the flabby superstar get back in shape. He had Best making daily five-mile runs and put him on a special diet that cut out bread, potatoes, sugar and milk. The Irishman made his first appearance of the year in early October when Ajax Amsterdam visited Old Trafford for Denis Law's testimonial, but he clearly still lacked fitness.

Tommy Docherty had promised to rejuvenate United, but his decision to gamble on Best hinted that the manager was close to desperation in his attempts to inject some life into his team. At the annual meeting of shareholders at Old Trafford on 9 October 1973, the directors announced a loss of £390,000 on the previous year. On the night before, in front of just 23,000 home fans, Docherty's expensively assembled side had gone out of the League Cup to Second Division Middlesbrough.

Things soon got worse. Lou Macari, who had been performing poorly, was fined £400 and transfer-listed by Docherty after refusing to turn out in a reserve match at Mossley. Macari had scored just five goals since joining United and had yet to hit the net in the current season. In late 1973, Ian Storey-Moore, who had been battling an ankle ligament injury for a year, was forced to quit football at the age of 28.

Docherty still had the chance to play his wild card – George Best. He was finally recalled to

Lou Macari

league action against Birmingham City on 20 October, as was Macari. A bearded Best had obviously lost pace while gaining weight. Still, his touches and his passing were in a healthy condition as United achieved their first league victory in five games. Goalkeeper Alex Stepney, now United's penalty taker, scored from the spot for the only goal of the game.

Sadly, United's form, and attendances, continued to dip. A 2–1 defeat by Sheffield United two days after Christmas plunged them into the third from bottom position in the table. That season, for the first time, three clubs were to be relegated from the First Division.

A 3–0 defeat at Queen's Park Rangers on New Year's Day 1974 heralded Best's first absence from training since his return. For several days, neither Docherty nor Crerand heard from the player. The following Saturday he was dropped for the Cup tie against Plymouth Argyle. In Docherty's mind, Best was no longer worth the trouble he generated and when he again failed to turn up for training in the week following the Cup tie, his time at Old Trafford had finally expired. "I have more important things on my mind than George Best," said Docherty. "My concern is in looking after the first team and running club affairs."

Best was put on the transfer list and suspended by the club for a fortnight. He emerged to say, "I will never play in a league match in this country again. I know that I have lost forever that certain spark that set me apart from other players and I also know that I can never get it back."

There was a further sign of strife when Bill Foulkes, the reserve team coach, was sent home from Old Trafford by Docherty in late January 1974.

Docherty continually chopped and changed his team but to no avail. A 2–0 defeat by Leeds United in February 1974 deposited United at

October 1973
Tommy Docherty's side are knocked out of the League Cup by Second Division Middlesbrough.

December 1973
A 2–1 defeat by Sheffield United two days after Christmas plunges the Reds into the relegation zone.

January 1974
Docherty places George Best on the transfer list. Best announces that he will never play a league match in England again.

MANCHESTER UNITED **OFFICIAL MEMBERS' HISTORY BOOK**   81

Following the nightmare relegation season of 1973/74, Tommy Docherty led United straight back up to the First Division.

the bottom of the league table and the previously unthinkable prospect of relegation was now at the forefront of everybody's minds. Alex Stepney, 1968 European Cup-winning hero, remained rational about the situation though:

"There's a fair chance we'll go down, but it's not the end of the world," he said. "It might take a couple of years to build again and get back into the First Division but we can do it. Others have and they aren't Manchester United. "Manchester United aren't just a club, they are an institution. It doesn't mean they can't have bad times, but they'd still be Manchester United, no matter what division they're in. No matter what people say or what they write about us, the spirit at Old Trafford is just as good as when we were doing well. We've got a good boss, good staff, some promising youngsters and the directors are behind us."

By late March 1974, United were seven points adrift of safety, but a Willie Morgan-inspired 3–1 win over Chelsea at Stamford Bridge offered hope. A 3–3 draw with Burnley moved them into the second from bottom spot, above Norwich City, whom they faced

next at Carrow Road. Inspired goalkeeping by Alex Stepney kept the Norwich forwards out and goals from Macari and young Brian Greenhoff gave United a 2–0 win, continuing the revival. On the train journey home the manager mingled freely with United supporters and promised them that if United did go down they would be back in the First Division the following season.

Stewart Houston, a £55,000 full-back signed from Brentford in December 1973, was working well with fellow Scottish defenders Forsyth, Buchan and Holton. Jim McCalliog, a Scottish international signed for £60,000 in March 1974, had teamed up with Greenhoff to form a useful midfield pairing. Morgan and Gerry Daly, a 19-year-old who had cost £12,000 from Bohemians a year previously, were making things happen on the wings. With Macari and 19-year-old youth product Sammy McIlroy a sharp-witted front two, there was now a very nice balance about the United team.

Despite the club's predicament, Docherty had abandoned his previous stifling tactics, which had included the occasional use of a

TIMELINE

February 1974
A 2–0 defeat at Leeds United deposits United at the bottom of the league table.

April 1974
United lose their penultimate league game 1–0 to Manchester City. Elsewhere Birmingham beat Norwich 2–1 and United are relegated.

May 1974
Striker Stuart Pearson signs from Hull City for £200,000.

82   MANCHESTER UNITED **OFFICIAL MEMBERS' HISTORY BOOK**

lone striker. Busby had suggested to Docherty that if United were to go down, they should do so in some style. It now looked possible that an expansive approach might even be rewarded with salvation from relegation.

Spirited victories over Newcastle United and Everton took United to within three points of fourth-bottom Southampton so United travelled to the Dell in late April 1974 knowing that a win would take them out of the relegation zone.

At Southampton, a patient display yielded results when McCalliog put United 1–0 up with a 20th-minute penalty, but a Mick Channon equalizer made the final score 1–1. With three games to play, United still had games in hand on Birmingham City and Southampton, the two sides immediately above them, but a midweek defeat at Everton – United's first in seven matches – cloaked Old Trafford in gloom.

United's penultimate match of the season was against Manchester City at Old Trafford and Denis Law, now captain at City, was given a tremendous welcome back by United fans.

United pressed into attack from the start and had two goal-bound efforts cleared off the City line but the game remained goalless until nine minutes from time. Then Law stuck out a heel to divert the ball past Alex Stepney.

"I didn't particularly want to go there and win the game," said Law. "It was 0–0 and then Franny Lee crossed the ball. I hadn't a clue where the goal was. I backheeled it and it was a complete fluke. It was an awful moment. I was very sad. In fact, that turned out to be my last kick of a ball in league football."

The goal signalled a mass pitch invasion and it took the police seven minutes to clear the playing area of hundreds of United fans who were hoping their actions would bring about an abandonment and a replay. Missiles rained down when the players reappeared and then,

Sammy McIlroy

despite Sir Matt Busby's tannoyed appeals for calm, a second pitch invasion sent the players to the dressing-rooms once more. Four minutes still remained to be played but when referee David Smith heard that Birmingham City had beaten Norwich 2–1, he knew that the outcome of the Old Trafford match was irrelevant and he kept the players inside.

A myth has since developed that Law's goal sent United down but it was Birmingham's victory that meant the Reds would be playing Second Division football for the first time in 37 years.

"We have the best supporters in the world," said Busby in the aftermath of the pitch invasion, "but a small number of them have done our name so much harm."

Even in the Second Division, the hooligans stalked United. In their opening game at Orient, there was another pitch invasion, and a linesman had to be replaced after being cut on the leg by a missile thrown from the terraces. Morgan made a more positive contribution to United's relaunch, chipping Orient goalkeeper John Jackson after half an hour. Houston's header from McIlroy's free-kick made for a steady 2–0 start.

Stuart Pearson, a £200,000 signing from Hull City in May 1974, was the only significant addition to the team. Two-footed, useful in the air and the possessor of superb reflexes, Pearson was a fine striker and the focal point of United's attacks. He would go on to finish the season with 18 goals. As had been suggested by their form in the latter stages of the 1973/74 season, United looked too good for the Second Division. Four wins out of four put them top of the table at the end of August 1974. Docherty's brisk, lively team were unbeaten until a 2–0 defeat at Norwich City in late September, but that still left them three points clear at the top.

By November 1974, Sunderland were United's closest challengers for promotion and

August 1974
United win their first game of the season in the Second Division, beating Leyton Orient 2–0 at Brisbane Road.

November 1974
United's closest league challengers Sunderland visit Old Trafford. United win a thriller 3–2 in front of 60,585 fans.

December 1974
Defender Jim Holton suffers a broken leg in a 4–4 draw at Sheffield Wednesday, an injury that was to end his United career.

when the Wearsiders visited Old Trafford that month, 5,000 fans were locked out of the ground. The 60,585 who did get in saw a tremendous game end in a 3–2 win for United, stretching their lead at the top to six points. Some of the rough edges had been knocked off Holton as part of United's reformed, refined style but, sadly, he suffered a broken leg in a 4–4 draw at Sheffield Wednesday on 7 December that was to end his United career.

Spiked fences nine foot high had been installed at the front of the terraces at Old Trafford after the pitch invasion against Manchester City, but the club was still plagued by hooliganism. At Hillsborough, pitch invasions led to 105 arrests.

"What can we do?" said Docherty. "We have a minority of supporters who are a disgrace. Every club has one or two troublemakers among their supporters but because of the size of our following the problem is bigger for us than for any other club."

It led to a new policy whereby United's away games were made all-ticket with the only point of sale for their fans being Old Trafford. That way, United supporters could be segregated.

United had made little impact in cup competition since the days of Wilf McGuinness, but a fine League Cup run took them to the 1975 semi-finals. Pearson was missing with a hamstring injury for the first leg of the semi with Norwich in January 1975, when 58,000 Old Trafford fans saw two dinky goals from Macari – one a sweet overhead kick – match two from Norwich's Ted MacDougall in a 2–2 draw. Pearson also missed the second leg in which United fell to a 1–0 defeat.

In the early weeks of 1975, United faltered slightly, as might have been expected of a side with an average age of 22. At times this team of quick, light players tended to look fragile and they were being tested to their limits. As Docherty said, "All the teams in this division

Steve Coppell

have played as well as they possibly can against us, simply to try to beat Manchester United."

His team had the character to remain on top throughout, though, and they ended the season as Second Division champions, three points clear of second-placed Aston Villa.

There was little change in policy or personnel for United's return to the First Division. The emphasis remained on attack. Wingers Daly and Steve Coppell (a signing from Tranmere Rovers during the 1974/75 season) together with attacking midfielder Macari spurred on the Red Devils' attacks and McIlroy and Pearson were the devilish duo up front. In defence, Jimmy Nicholl took over from Forsyth as the regular right-back early in the 1975/76 season while Greenhoff moved back to partner Buchan in central defence.

Docherty was modest in his ambitions for the 1975/76 season, stating that he would be happy merely to finish outside of the bottom three, but his side's sumptuous attacking football propelled them to the top of the table. United were a slick, cohesive unit, thoroughly familiar with each other's play. Throughout the autumn of 1975, United and QPR took turns at leading the First Division. Competition at the top was tight and when United lost 3–1 to Liverpool at Anfield in November, despite having played with wonderful flair, they slipped to fifth.

Docherty remained confident enough to raise his sights, stating that he hoped his team would finish high enough in the league to win a place in European competition. He further strengthened his team in late 1975 by signing outside-left Gordon Hill from Millwall for £70,000. Daly made way for him by switching from the left wing to central midfield.

Two days before Christmas, United went top again. A stunning overhead kick from Macari just inside the penalty area earned them a 1–1 draw at Everton in a match that was held up for

January 1975
United's fine League Cup run is ended at the semi-final stage by Norwich City who win 3–2 on aggregate.

February 1975
Winger Steve Coppell signs from Tranmere Rovers for £60,000.

April 1975
United end the season as Second Division champions, three points clear of second-placed Aston Villa.

84   MANCHESTER UNITED **OFFICIAL MEMBERS' HISTORY BOOK**

15 minutes when the Goodison Park floodlights failed. On Boxing Day, Liverpool resumed their leadership of the First Division, but United were back on top in January 1976. That month, Pat Crerand left the staff; Tommy Cavanagh was now Docherty's assistant.

United remained in contention for the title and a thrilling FA Cup run took them to the final, putting them in with the chance of the Double. Not since the 1956/57 season had United been faced with such a pleasant prospect. Docherty had fielded an unchanged team for 18 successive matches from December 1975 to March 1976 and there was a smooth understanding between his players.

"Our players have this bad habit – they keep passing the ball to members of their own side," he joked.

A crowd of 61,879 – United's biggest for six years – saw a 2–1 win over Everton keep United in the title hunt but four days later, Stoke City crept away from Old Trafford with a 1–0 win thanks to a breakaway goal three minutes from time. United's attacking style always left them vulnerable to the counter-attack and that defeat ended the Old Trafford side's brave challenge for the 1975/76 title. They finished third, four points behind champions Liverpool.

"I have never been with a team that is so calm," said Docherty as he turned his thoughts to the Wembley Cup final. United didn't train in the week before the final – the manager believed that after a full season's games they were as fit as they would ever be and well aware of what was required of them.

One of Docherty's characteristics was to criticize other clubs and players publicly. Prior to United's FA Cup semi-final with Derby County, he had said, "This is the first time a Cup final will be played at Hillsborough. The other semi-final is a bit of a joke really." That match, between Second Division Southampton and Third Division Crystal Palace, ended in a 2–0 win for the south coast club who had doubtless taken note of Docherty's words. United had stuttered and stalled in the weeks

The teams walk out for the 1976 FA Cup final, in which underdogs Southampton shocked United, winning 1–0.

before the final and Southampton's coaching staff had carefully scrutinized all of their matches. At Wembley, the experienced Saints defenders shackled United's sparky forwards with maximum efficiency. Southampton created the greater number of chances and only a point-blank save by Stepney prevented Mick Channon giving Southampton a first-half lead. After an hour, in a rare United attack, McIlroy leapt to head Hill's corner off the crossbar. With just five minutes remaining, McCalliog, discarded by Docherty a year earlier, slipped a super pass through the middle of the United defence. Bobby Stokes glided on to the ball and from 20 yards placed a first-time, left-footed shot on the run past Stepney for the only goal of the game. Docherty could only look on wistfully as Southampton celebrated with the Cup.

It was a disappointing end to a distinguished season, but United had plenty to look forward to as the 1976/77 fixtures began, in particular a return to European competition after an

September 1975
Newly-promoted United win five and draw one of their first six matches to go top of Division One.

November 1975
Left winger Gordon Hill signs from Millwall for £70,000.

December 1975
Two days before Christmas, United go top of the First Division again after a 1-1 draw with Everton at Goodison Park.

absence of eight seasons. Their UEFA Cup place, as reward for third position in the league, produced a first-round tie with Ajax.

The first leg was played at the Olympic Stadium, Amsterdam. United's supporters were quarantined by empty terraces all around them in their section of the ground. A goal by sweeper Ruud Krol, when he eased past four United defenders, gave Ajax the only goal of the game.

In the return, watched by 59,000, a Macari goal levelled the tie shortly before half-time and midway through the second half McIlroy's strike put United into the second round. An even more difficult task presented itself when they were drawn against Juventus. By coincidence, Manchester City had faced the Italians in the first round, losing 2–1 on aggregate. Tony Book, City's manager, offered to assist United by giving his observations on Juventus but Docherty responded, "I will not seek advice from anyone outside my own staff."

At the time of the draw United were once again top of the First Division, but by 20 October 1976, when they met Juventus, they had dropped to eighth, although still only two points behind leaders Liverpool.

At Old Trafford, Juventus's calculating, high-grade football brought them several good scoring opportunities early in the match but it remained goalless for the first half hour. Then a cross from Nicholl was headed on by Coppell and dropped for Hill, leaning back, to steer a sharp volley past goalkeeper Dino Zoff. There was no further scoring although the rest of the match was littered with vicious fouls and off-the-ball incidents.

Buchan was injured for both legs and his composure was badly missed in the Stadio Comunale, Turin, where 65,000 Juventus fans roared on their team. It was United who made the best early chance when Hill's diving header from Coppell's cross went narrowly wide of Zoff's post. At the back, United kept Juventus out for the opening half hour. Then a swift four-man move ended with Roberto

The glory days are here again: jubilant United players celebrate the 2–1 victory over Liverpool in the 1977 FA Cup final.

TIMELINE

April 1976 United beat Derby County 2–0 at Hillsborough to reach the FA Cup final.

May 1976 United suffer a shock 1–0 defeat by Southampton in the FA Cup final and finish third in the league, just four points behind champions Liverpool.

November 1976 United lose 3–0 to Juventus at the Stadio Comunale in the UEFA Cup second round second leg, and slip out of the competition 3–1 on aggregate.

Boninsegna sweeping the ball into the United net. Midway through the second half, Boninsegna met Marco Tardelli's cross with a neat flick to put Juventus ahead in the tie. The Italians made sure of their progress when, in the final minutes, Romeo Benetti crashed a shot past Stepney.

By November, United were rooted in mid-table in the league and young wingers Coppell and Hill were starting to look jaded. United played 4–2–4 when attacking, with the full-backs pushed up in support of the wingers, but they reverted to 4-4-2 when the opposition had the ball, with the wingers carrying out defensive duties. It was a heavy burden for such young players and Docherty rested Hill, switching Coppell to the left wing.

Stuart Pearson

A series of indifferent results meant that the league title was already out of reach by Christmas. United diverted all their energies towards the FA Cup and extracted a measure of revenge on Southampton by defeating the holders on their way to the final.

On 21 May, 100,000 fans packed Wembley to see United take on Liverpool, who were chasing an unprecedented European Cup, league and FA Cup treble.

Liverpool had the better of the first half, and with both Steve Coppell and Gordon Hill subdued on the wings, United had just one goal attempt, a weak effort by Stuart Pearson.

Five minutes after the restart, United took the lead with their first serious attempt on target. Sammy McIlroy's centre-circle header deceived Liverpool captain Emlyn Hughes and Jimmy Greenhoff, a recent signing from Stoke City, headed the ball on past Tommy Smith. It fell neatly into Stuart Pearson's path. Pearson coolly nodded the ball on and teed himself up to pelt a right-foot volley past Clemence.

The lead lasted two minutes. Jimmy Case, with his back to Buchan on the edge of the United area, controlled Jones's pass on his thigh, took another touch, then turned quickly to hit a fine spinning shot towards goal. Stepney got a hand to it but couldn't prevent the ball racing into the net.

Three minutes later, the Reds responded with what proved to be the Cup-clinching goal. Jimmy Nicholl's long, high ball forward was nodded on by Lou Macari, who beat Hughes in the air. Jimmy Greenhoff tussled with Smith for the ball and when it bounced clear to Macari, his stabbed shot looked as though it was going wide until it took a deflection off Jimmy Greenhoff's midriff and the ball veered crazily past Clemence.

United were forced to defend for most of the remainder of the game. Tommy Docherty sat anxiously chewing gum on the bench, nervously glancing at his watch before it was finally over and United had won the Cup for the first time since 1963.

For Docherty, the high was short-lived; on 4 July 1977, just six weeks after victory in the Cup final, Docherty was sacked when his affair with Mary Brown, wife of club physiotherapist Laurie Brown, was made public.

In a rare contemplative moment, Docherty had once said, "A manager of any football club is a lonely individual. He has many associates but few genuine friends. At least we know where we stand."

He had counted Matt Busby among those friends and had hoped that Busby and the United board would stand by him after his affair with Mary Brown was revealed. They didn't and it seemed strange that Docherty, this tough, streetwise Glaswegian, should be brought low as a result of a love affair.

"I have been punished for falling in love," he said. "What I have done has nothing at all to do with my track record as a manager."

Docherty had exchanged his love affair with United for personal happiness. A new chapter in United's history was about to begin.

March 1977
United gain revenge on Southampton, beating them 2–1 in an FA Cup fifth-round replay

May 1977
Goals from Stuart Pearson and Jimmy Greenhoff clinch a 2–1 victory over Liverpool in the FA Cup final at Wembley.

July 1977
On 4 July 1977, Tommy Docherty is sacked after his affair with the club physio's wife is made public.

Following Tommy Docherty's shock sacking,
Dave Sexton took over as Manchester United
manager in summer 1977.

CHAPTER TEN

THE SEXTON PRINCIPLE

New manager Dave Sexton relaxed by reading poetry and philosophy, and applied a thoughtful approach to football, emphasising technique and tactics over pure inspiration... but would United fans approve?

anchester United had to move quickly once the decision had been made to dismiss Tommy Docherty as manager. The first fixtures of the 1977/78 season were fast approaching and as the players returned from holiday to begin pre-season training in July 1977, moves were afoot to land Docherty's successor.

Within days one of the prominent candidates for the job, Dave Sexton, had negotiated his release from his contract as manager of Queen's Park Rangers. Sexton had been expected to leave Loftus Road over the summer to join Arsenal as a coach, but when United invited him to become manager at Old Trafford he eagerly accepted. Eight days after Docherty's dismissal, Sexton was in place as the new Manchester United manager.

Forty-seven-year old Sexton had managed Leyton Orient and Chelsea (where he won the 1970 FA Cup and 1971 European Cup Winners' Cup) before QPR (with whom he nearly won the First Division title in 1975/76) and was an ultra-modern manager. An admirer of Hennes Weismuller, the meticulous coach of Borussia Monchengladbach, Sexton spliced together home-made coaching videos for his players and frequently travelled to expand his knowledge of the game. In his spare time, he relaxed by reading the work of American poet Robert Frost and philosopher Ludwig Wittgenstein – fairly unusual leisure pursuits for a football manager.

On a three-game summer tour of Norway with Sexton in charge, United scored 21 goals;

and they played their part in an absorbing 0–0 draw with Liverpool in the Charity Shield match in August.

The unexpected nature of Docherty's departure, allied to the short space of time between the new appointment and the start of the season, meant that Sexton had no chance to make personnel changes in summer and the existing squad of players warmed to him. "How could anyone not like him?" said Lou Macari after United beat Birmingham City 4–1 on the opening day of the season.

The team that day at St Andrews was almost the same as the Cup-winning one; the only change was that David McCreery played in place of Jimmy Greenhoff, who had been injured during the Charity Shield match. The team's explosive style remained intact. Macari scored a hat-trick against Birmingham and he said afterwards, "People say that we're apt to go flat during a game but at the pace we play we need a quiet period to get our second wind."

United went on to garner a series of mixed results that meant they were in the top half of the First Division table as they prepared to meet St Etienne in the European Cup Winners' Cup first round on 14 September 1977.

Thirty seven United supporters ended up in hospital after violent confrontations with St Etienne fans on the terraces shortly before the first-leg match was due to begin. The bulk of the United supporters inside the Stade Geoffroy Guichard had found that their tickets admitted them to the terracing behind a goal where they were surrounded by French fans.

TIMELINE

August 1977
Dave Sexton enjoys his first league victory as manager of Manchester United, a 4–1 win at Birmingham City on the opening day of the 1977/78 season.

September 1977
Crowd trouble flares during United's 1–1 draw with St Etienne in the European Cup Winners' Cup, and UEFA expel the Reds from the competition...

October 1977
... On appeal, United are reinstated and the second leg is played at Plymouth Argyle's ground. United win 2–0 to clinch a 3–1 aggregate victory.

MANCHESTER UNITED **OFFICIAL MEMBERS' HISTORY BOOK**   89

Giant defender Gordon McQueen, who joined United in January 1978, combined elegant defensive play with an eye for goal.

Pushing and jostling developed into a full-scale battle that led to French riot police, who had anticipated trouble, wading in with batons.

Chairman Louis Edwards later commented, "I saw innocent people beaten down by police. When our supporters misbehave I am the first to condemn them, but this was not one of those occasions. They were the victims."

For a while there were doubts whether the match would go ahead. But when the game got under way, United players put on a smooth show of attacking football, Gordon Hill scoring their goal in a 1–1 draw.

However, five days later, Manchester United were expelled from the competition by UEFA.

A week later, on Monday 26 September, Louis Edwards, Sir Matt Busby, Les Olive and Denzil Haroun, a United director, made the club's appeal to UEFA's disciplinary committee in Zurich, Switzerland. They put the case to UEFA that St Etienne's lack of supporter segregation had sparked the violence. UEFA responded by reducing United's punishment to a £7,500 fine and ruled that they should play their second leg a minimum of 125 miles from Manchester.

The second leg would now take place on 5 October, a week later than scheduled. Aberdeen was the club's preferred choice of venue, but the date didn't suit Aberdeen FC so the game was switched to Plymouth.

Ticket distribution ensured that the bulk of the crowd would be neutral – Plymouth Argyle FC sold 20,000 tickets to their own supporters. A 31,634 crowd at Home Park saw United, nonplussed by the fuss surrounding the tie, overwhelm the French side, with goals from Pearson and Coppell clinching a 3–1 aggregate win.

A fortnight later, United were in another port, Oporto, facing Portuguese Cup-winners Porto. This first leg of their second-round tie took place in front of 70,000 of Porto's fervent followers in the Estadio Das Antas. United's following was restricted to 160, each of whom had been stringently vetted by the club, and they saw the Reds subside to a dismal 4–0 defeat. United's Cup Winners' Cup hopes seemed to have been dashed before a ball had been kicked in the second leg.

TIMELINE

November 1977
Despite a brave 5–2 win at home to Porto, United lose 6–5 on aggregate and are eliminated from the Cup Winners' Cup.

January 1978
Sexton signs striker Joe Jordan from Leeds United for £350,000 – a month later he again raids Elland Road to buy central defender Gordon McQueen for £495,000.

April 1978
United end the 1977/78 season in 10th position, 22 points behind champions Nottingham Forest.

A second 4–0 defeat in three days, at West Bromwich Albion the following Saturday, once again exposed United's lack of a dominant centre-half. In addition, Stepney was clearly reaching the end of his career. When United lost 2–1 at Aston Villa a week later, it left the club 13th in the First Division and already out of contention for the title.

"We're a cup side," said Macari. "We're not consistent enough over 42 league games."

United were without both Macari and Brian Greenhoff, both of whom were injured, for the return with FC Porto, but they had the support of 53,000 Old Trafford fans as they began their uphill task. With seven minutes gone, Coppell turned swiftly on the edge of the penalty area to shoot and score the opener. United rode into attack after attack, but they were stung by a Porto counter-attack from which Seninho equalized on the half hour.

Murca put through his own goal five minutes before half-time and Jimmy Nicholl cracked a shot into the Porto net shortly before the break to make it 3–1 on the night.

Midway through the second period Coppell, from close range, made it 4–1, but United were undone when Seninho again rounded off another breakaway five minutes from time with his and Porto's second goal. A second own goal by Murca ended the scoring, making it 5–2 to United on the night but 6–5 to Porto on aggregate. United were cheered off the pitch by their supporters after their valiant but ultimately fruitless victory.

The credit gained by that performance soon evaporated. United suffered their fourth league defeat in five games – 2–1 to Arsenal – the following Saturday, leaving them eighth from bottom of the First Division, two points above the relegation places. Another defeat, 2–1 at Nottingham Forest a week later, emphasized their plight.

"Recent results have been very cruel to us.," said Sexton. "We have been without players of the calibre of Lou Macari, James Greenhoff and Brian Greenhoff, to name three. Nothing is wrong that a couple of wins will not put right though."

A Stuart Pearson goal in a 1–0 win over Norwich City in late November 1977 brought Sexton some relief and United slowly but steadily made their way up the table from then onwards. The modest revival in their fortunes was not strong enough to prevent the FA Cup-holders exiting the tournament in the fourth round after a replay against West Bromwich Albion. They ended the 1977/78 season in 10th position, 22 points behind champions Nottingham Forest.

By then, Sexton had started to ring the changes. Alex Stepney had been replaced in goal by Paddy Roche, while a combined total of over £800,000 had been spent bringing striker Joe Jordan and centre-half Gordon McQueen (both Scottish internationals) from Leeds United to Old Trafford.

United had lacked a dominant centre-half since the days of Jim Holton, and at six foot four inches tall and thirteen-and-a-half stone McQueen would become Holton's true successor. There would be few finer sights at Old Trafford in the late sventies than McQueen, with his distinctive mane of blond hair, rising majestically to head the ball clear. Not only that, he also had speed plus exceptional close control for a big man, and frequently roved forward to score and set up goals.

Joe Jordan

Joe Jordan didn't score in his first two months at United, but the ferociously committed six-foot-tall target man was welcomed by his team-mates.

"He gives us the get-out of a high ball into the middle, which we never had before," said Steve Coppell. "It has been drilled into us that we must play football right into the penalty area and get to the line, keeping our crosses low. Now we have more options."

August 1976
United's centenary is marked by a friendly game against Real Madrid.

November 1978
Twenty-year old Ipswich-born South African keeper Gary Bailey makes his United debut against Ipswich Town. It is the first of 85 consecutive appearances.

March 1979
Only 36,085 turn up at Old Trafford for the match against Leeds United, the club's smallest attendance since the Reds returned to the First Division in 1975.

Old Trafford crowds thinned considerably in the spring of 1978 as United ambled towards the end of the season. By then, Sexton had made the significant decision to sell Gordon Hill to Derby County for £250,000. From now on, United would play with just one winger. Hill's move prompted an exchange of insults. He claimed there was a serious lack of team spirit at Old Trafford. He also attacked Sexton's methods, stating, "You need an O-level or a degree to understand the tactics at Old Trafford." Sexton responded, "Hill is a very selfish player. The other lads have had to do a lot of work to accommodate him."

Sexton's other winger, Steve Coppell, was more supportive of his manager. "Injuries mean we've been unable to consolidate the work that Dave Sexton is putting in," he said. "We never had tactical talks with Tommy Docherty. We had a set way of playing and we improvised around that. We never discussed other teams before we played them. The changes have not been too extensive, but what has been done has tended to involve the players more. It is appreciated and that will soon begin to show through our results."

The centenary of United's founding under the name Newton Heath was marked at the beginning of the 1978/79 season when Real Madrid provided the opposition for a match at Old Trafford. Goalkeeper Alex Stepney was given a guard of honour by the directors and players as he took to the turf before the game – it would be his last major appearance as a United player. Bobby Charlton, Johnny Carey, Jimmy Delaney and other prominent figures from the past also took a bow before kick-off. Stepney saved a Pirri penalty, and Sammy McIlroy and Jimmy Greenhoff each scored twice as United won 4–0 in front of 50,000 fans. It was a heartening overture to the season.

Stuart Pearson had undergone a cartilage operation so Jimmy Greenhoff partnered Jordan in attack. United were now using a more measured style under Sexton and goals proved hard to come by. In the autumn of 1978, four successive 1–1 draws reflected their unspectacular progress. That, in combination with a 2–1 home defeat by Watford in the League Cup in early October, meant Old Trafford crowds continued to tumble. United used a 4–4–2 system, with Coppell still wide on the right but he was now being deployed more in midfield rather than as an attacking winger. It was a stuffy style that knocked much of the excitement out of United's play.

After another 1–1 draw, with Southampton in November 1978, Sexton's team were booed from the pitch at Old Trafford. Sexton's popularity plummeted even further after a 5–1 defeat at Birmingham City later that month. It had been six years since United had conceded five goals in one match.

Louis Edwards responded by promising Sexton £1 million for players – the money would be raised by a share issue that Edwards proposed for later in the year. Sexton wasted little time in entering the transfer market. Within hours he had made a £440,000 offer for Jim Blyth of Coventry City, but Blyth failed the medical. It would have been a record fee for a goalkeeper but the move was puzzling as Blyth had been in Coventry's reserves for weeks, attempting to recover from the serious back injury that had vetoed the transfer.

The following Saturday Paddy Roche, who had been between the sticks for the 5–1 defeat at Birmingham, found himself replaced by Gary Bailey, a 20-year-old, Ipswich-born South African making his United debut.

Bailey's form was so impressive that his confident debut, in a 2–0 home win over Ipswich Town, proved to be the first of 85 consecutive first-team appearances. For the following eight seasons, he was United's first-

April 1979
United beat Liverpool 1–0 in an FA Cup semi-final replay at Goodison Park, after a 2–2 thriller at Maine Road. Jimmy Greenhoff heads the winning goal.

May 1979
United finish ninth in the league, 23 points behind champions Liverpool. The Reds are also beaten 3–2 by Arsenal in an FA Cup final thriller.

August 1978
Twenty-two-year-old Ray Wilkins joins United from Chelsea for a £750,000 fee.

92   MANCHESTER UNITED OFFICIAL MEMBERS' HISTORY BOOK

Gary Bailey

Dave Sexton watches from the dug-out at West Brom's Hawthorns ground. In the background sits his eventual successor Ron Atkinson.

choice goalkeeper. Instead of purchasing a keeper, Sexton signed Mickey Thomas, a left-sided midfielder, from Wrexham for £300,000.

Louis Edwards's son Martin, 33 in 1978, now had 1,904 United shares, nearly twice as many as the total held by the rest of the United board. Members of the Edwards family held 75 per cent of United's 3,678 shares. Under the proposed share issue, one million new shares were to be issued at an Extraordinary General Meeting to be held on 18 December 1978. Louis Edwards and Martin Edwards would take up the full number of new shares to which they were entitled at a cost of around £750,000, doubling their shareholding in the club.

On the field, United entered the New Year once again well out of contention for the title and out of the League Cup. The fans were losing patience with Sexton. Results were mediocre and United's style was dull. In March 1979, there were 36,085 at Old Trafford for a match with Leeds United, the club's smallest attendance for a league match since they had returned to the First Division in 1975.

"We're a young team in transition and we're still learning," insisted Sexton. "We always play with a lot of spirit. We've got a good, fighting squad and there's also a lot of skill there. I have the same aspirations as the crowd, although I have had it brought home to me this season that winning is not enough if we don't win well."

In the second half of the season, United concentrated all their energies on the FA Cup and reached the semi-finals, where they faced a Liverpool side already certain of the title. The Anfield club would eventually finish the 1978/79 season 23 points ahead of ninth-placed United in the First Division. The game was played at Maine Road. Liverpool were unbeaten in 16 matches and had conceded only three goals in those games. United had conceded seven goals in their previous three matches – a win, a defeat and a draw – but they ignored the form, taking a 2–1 lead through goals by Brian Greenhoff and Joe Jordan. Alan Hansen scored a rare goal to equalize five minutes from time.

"It was as though we had lost," said Martin Buchan. "We had had the feeling that this was going to be our day. It was very disappointing not to win. Now, an hour after the match, the spirit in the dressing-room is reviving."

In the replay at Goodison Park four days later, United sped into attack, pressing

September 1979
United start the 1979/80 season promisingly with four wins and two draws and by mid-September they are top of Division One.

December 1979
By Christmas, United and Liverpool are equal on points, six clear of the nearest challengers, but when the two teams meet on Boxing Day, Liverpool gain a comfortable 2–0 win at Anfield.

January 1980
United sign 27-year-old Yugoslavia international centre-half Nikola Jovanovic from Red Star Belgrade for £300,000. Jovanovic is United's first-ever foreign player.

Steve Coppell battles for the ball in the 1979 FA Cup final.

ball into the net. Two minutes later, McIlroy pursued a difficult ball, twisted past three opponents and stretched to nick an equalizer just as the ball appeared to have finally eluded his control.

Arsenal attacked from the restart and Liam Brady burst down United's right flank, passing to Graham Rix. His cross found Alan Sunderland who nicked Arsenal's winner at the back post. Less than a minute had passed since McIlroy's goal. The cruelty of the climax left Sir Matt Busby in tears at the final whistle.

Sexton maintained that United could challenge for the title in the 1979/80 season. "These are super lads," he said of his players. "They know they're at the number-one club. You look around the walls at Old Trafford and see photographs of the great sides. My job is to get this side up on the walls and then nobody would remember our struggles. Believe it or not, this is the enjoyable part for me. Any success is preceded by a struggle and the struggle is the fun."

The manager added £750,000 midfielder Ray Wilkins to his squad shortly before the season began. At 18, Wilkins had become the youngest-ever captain of Chelsea. Five years on, following Chelsea's relegation from the First Division, United fought off rival bids from Everton and Ipswich to bring him to Old Trafford. Sexton was delighted:

"Ray will be our link between attack and defence and I'm sure he'll help our strikers, because he has the ability to pinpoint passes. He's a midfield general."

Offsetting the purchase of Wilkins, Brian Greenhoff went to Leeds United for £350,000, Stuart Pearson to West Ham United for £220,000 and David McCreery was offloaded to QPR for £200,000.

Wilkins, McIlroy and Thomas now made up the midfield, with Coppell as a deep-lying winger. Macari had returned to the attack, alongside Jordan. Nicholl and Arthur Albiston were the regular full-backs, with McQueen and Buchan the central defenders who protected goalkeeper Bailey.

Liverpool back with some superb attacking play. A host of chances resulted, culminating in a Joe Jordan header that smacked off the crossbar before being scrambled clear. When a goal failed to follow, Liverpool came into the game and Ray Kennedy hit Bailey's bar with a headed effort. Twelve minutes from time, Jimmy Greenhoff stylishly stole on to Thomas's cross to head the ball, on the bounce, past Ray Clemence, taking United into their third final in four years.

The Reds' opponents at Wembley were Arsenal and tickets were changing hands for £300, 30 times their face value, in the hours before the match. United supporters who had not been struck dumb by those prices were rendered speechless by half-time as Arsenal took a 2–0 lead with goals from Brian Talbot and Frank Stapleton.

United toiled hard to get back into the game but no tangible reward arrived until the 87th minute when Jordan's low centre was met by McQueen sticking out a long left leg to jab the

TIMELINE

January 1980
United are beaten in the third round of the FA Cup by Tottenham Hotspur. After a 1–1 draw at White Hart Lane, Spurs win the replay 1–0 at Old Trafford.

February 1980
United chairman Louis Edwards passes away at the age of 65 after suffering a heart attack. His son Martin succeeds him.

March 1980
Ipswich trounce United 6–0 at Portman Road, the club's heaviest defeat for more than 19 years.

94   MANCHESTER UNITED **OFFICIAL MEMBERS' HISTORY BOOK**

By mid-September this settled line-up had started to work well as a unit and, with Wilkins at his playmaking best, United were top of the First Division. They swapped the top spot with Nottingham Forest throughout the autumn until, in November, Liverpool seized the lead.

United responded to that challenge with a fast, flowing 5–0 win over Norwich City that repositioned them at the top. Sexton described it as "football as it should be played; the best display of my time at Old Trafford".

By Christmas, Liverpool and United were equal on points and six points clear of the rest of the First Division. They met at Anfield on Boxing Day, but United were well beaten in a 2–0 defeat. "We just didn't play," said Jordan.

Sexton's first signing of the 1980s was Nikola Jovanovic. The 27-year-old Yugoslav, international centre-half cost £300,000 from Red Star Belgrade, and was United's first foreign player.

"It is marvellous for us to have such a player in his prime," said Sexton, "but he won't go into the first team straight away. He'll have to settle down domestically first."

Sadly, chairman Louis Edwards, passed away in February 1980 at the age of 65 after suffering a heart attack in the bath at his home in Cheshire. Matt Busby described the death as a tragedy for Manchester. Louis Edwards's son Martin succeeded him.

Although ushered out of the FA Cup in the third round by Tottenham Hotspur, United continued to chase Liverpool valiantly, but at the beginning of March they hit a low when they were thumped 6–0 at Ipswich, the club's heaviest defeat for more than 19 years.

The gap between Liverpool and United soon widened ominously to six points. In April, Sexton instructed his team to go all out for victories and they obliged, winning six games in succession to bring them, once again, level on points with Liverpool. The Merseysiders,

however, had a considerably better goal difference and a game in hand and when United lost their final match, at Leeds, while Liverpool were beating Aston Villa 4–1, the title went to Anfield. United ended the season two points behind Liverpool.

Before that dramatic denouement, Martin Edwards had awarded Sexton and his assistant Tommy Cavanagh new three-year contracts. "I am already looking forward to next season," said the delighted manager.

Unfortunately, the 1980/81 season proved to be unproductive. United fell at the first hurdle in the League Cup when they were knocked out by Coventry City. A month later they went out of the UEFA Cup in the first round on away goals after drawing 1–1 on aggregate with Polish side Widzew Lodz. A fourth-round FA Cup defeat at Nottingham Forest was embarrassing, since United had whisked away Forest's star striker Garry Birtles for a United record £1.25 million fee just three months earlier. Despite being United's first £1 million-plus player, Birtles scored just once in 28 appearances during the season. United finished eighth in the league.

Martin Buchan

In his four years at the club, Sexton had made radical changes to the Manchester United style. They were now by and large perceived as being a stuffy side, packing the midfield and as concerned about stopping the opposition playing as in playing themselves. It had been difficult for the Manchester United support to suffer this approach to the game even when the team were challenging for trophies. It was indefensible when it took the club nowhere.

Sexton was dismissed in the spring of 1981. By then, the Old Trafford fans had begun voting with their feet and were staying away in considerable numbers. They knew, if Sexton did not, that United demanded a much more expansive style than the one that he had been able to provide for them.

May 1980
United lose 2–0 to Leeds United at Elland Road in their last league fixture. Meanwhile Liverpool beat Aston Villa 4–1 to win the title by two points.

October 1980
United sign Nottingham Forest's star striker Garry Birtles for £1.25 million fee. Birtles is the club's first million pound signing, but he would score just once in 28 appearances during 1980/81.

April 1981
Dave Sexton is sacked, although the team win seven games in a row at the end of the season – the best run or results since Matt Busby was manager.

Match-winning goalscorer Norman Whiteside celebrates the 1985 FA Cup final win over Everton with Kevin Moran. This was one of two FA Cup successes during Ron Atkinson's managerial reign.

CHAPTER ELEVEN

BIG RON &
THE FA CUP

*Flamboyant new manager Big Ron Atkinson ushered in an era
of big-money transfers, fast-flowing play and exciting cup runs.
But the league championhip trophy remained lodged on Merseyside.*

The Manchester United that Ron Atkinson inherited at the outset of 1981/82 seemed set for a serious title challenge. They had ended the previous season by winning their last seven league matches but while such sprints to the finishing line are all well and good, Atkinson recognized that his team would need greater stamina and strength of character to perform throughout the course of a season.

Turning his attention to the midfield, Atkinson broke the British transfer record to buy Bryan Robson for £1.5 million. For good measure, he also signed Remi Moses. Both had played under Atkinson at his previous club, West Bromwich Albion.

Atkinson knew from experience that Robson was a born leader, prepared to stretch every sinew and break every bone in his body for the cause. "Robbo" would be the captain and inspiration of Atkinson's new United.

New players always create a buzz around a ground, but some of the established players also produced the goods for Atkinson. Sammy McIlroy scored a hat-trick against Wolves, ironically on the day that his eventual replacement, Bryan Robson, signed for United. Even Garry Birtles silenced his critics, not to mention a few comedians, when he brought his miserable goal drought to an overdue end. Previously the club's

Ron Atkinson

record signing, Birtles benefited from playing alongside Atkinson's first acquisition, Frank Stapleton.

"Frank was one of the best headers of the ball I'd ever seen," says Arthur Albiston, one of the United defenders retained by Ron Atkinson. "He would direct the ball into the net with his head like some people kick a ball. He was a great target man, great for us at the back because he'd make our passes look perfect."

While the new arrivals were exciting, Atkinson's first season was essentially one of transition. United did well to finish third in the league, but in the FA and League Cups they fell at the first hurdle.

Atkinson sold Sammy McIlroy to Stoke City, and in the summer of 1982 made one more change to his midfield, signing Arnold Muhren from Ipswich Town. Slotting in alongside three England internationals, the creative Dutchman completed one of the finest midfield quartets in the country.

"Arnold wasn't the quickest of players, but he had a fantastic brain and it was great for me to play with him on the left," recalls Albiston. "In the middle of the park, we had Robson and Ray Wilkins and on the right side we had Steve Coppell. He was a flying machine but he could also tuck in and help out. We had great balance in midfield."

The midfield still needed a forward who

TIMELINE

June 1981
Ron Atkinson is appointed the new manager of Manchester United FC.

August 1981
Atkinson signs his first player, striker Frank Stapleton from Arsenal for £900,000.

October 1981
Atkinson signs Bryan Robson from his former club West Bromwich Albion for £1.5 million, a British record transfer fee.

could put the finishing touches to their artistry. Atkinson took the advice of his "best-ever signing", youth coach Eric Harrison, and called up Norman Whiteside from the team that played in the 1982 FA Youth Cup final (losing to Watford 7–6 on aggregate).

Whiteside had been just 16 and still an apprentice when he'd made his first-team debut as a substitute against Brighton in April 1982. The Belfast teenager (who was discovered by Bob Bishop, the same talent scout who had found George Best) had the height and build of a much older man and adapted easily to first-team football.

While Stapleton scored in the first win of the 1982/83 season against Birmingham City, Norman netted in the second, third and fourth victories over Nottingham Forest, Everton and Ipswich Town. The two strikers, brought together from different sides of the Irish border, seemed to have formed the perfect partnership. But just as Atkinson got used to things going well, his dream team was broken up by an injury to Ray Wilkins. The United and England captain fractured a cheekbone in a League Cup game at Bournemouth and missed almost three months of action.

Although Remi Moses filled in well in terms of tenacity, the team missed the guile of Wilkins. League points were thrown away, and United eventually finished third for the second year running. Injuries had certainly thrown a spanner in the works, or as Arthur Albiston put it, "If we had played with a settled midfield for the whole season, I think things could have been different."

If the league was again a source of disappointment, the fans had plenty to cheer in the cups. In the FA Cup, United knocked out West Ham, Luton Town, Derby County and Everton in the early rounds. Meanwhile in the League Cup, sponsored by the Milk Marketing Board, the Reds beat Bournemouth and Bradford City

Bryan Robson

over two legs, then Southampton and Nottingham Forest in single ties.

So the twin towers of Wembley beckoned Atkinson's team on two fronts in the spring of 1983, but one obstacle remained, the same one in both competitions – Arsenal. The Gunners were almost the national stadium's resident club side, having played there in the FA Cup finals of 1978, 1979 and 1980. In 1979, they defeated United 3–2 in the final, with Stapleton among the Arsenal scorers. It seemed inevitable that he would eventually strike against his old club, and he did just that in the first leg of the League Cup semi-final on 15 February 1983. United won the match 4–2 at Highbury, thanks to Frank and the other scorers, Coppell (two) and Whiteside. After seeing out the second leg at Old Trafford (2–1; scorers: Moran and Coppell), the Reds were ready for Wembley, where they would meet the holders Liverpool.

Fans of the two biggest clubs in the north west descended on north London on 26 March 1983 for what would prove to be a classic League Cup final. United took the lead after only 12 minutes, with a brilliant goal by Whiteside. He turned Alan Hansen inside out before striking with his weaker right foot to become the youngest-ever player to score in a League Cup final.

For long periods afterwards United were well on top, but a 25-yarder by Liverpool left-back Alan Kennedy late on levelled the scores. Kennedy's equalizer was a cruel blow for United, and extra-time looked ominous for a side that had sustained two injuries in the heart of its defence.

"We ended up with Lou Macari and Frank Stapleton playing across the back four with myself and Mike Duxbury," remembers Albiston. "Big Gordon McQueen was injured and had to play on the right wing."

It was a makeshift defence but Liverpool still needed a special goal to beat United. After his

Arsenal's David O'Leary
looks on as Manchester
United's Norman Whiteside
smashes home the winner
in the 1983 FA Cup
semi-final.

attempted pass was blocked, Ronnie Whelan decided to shoot for himself and curled the ball perfectly around Gary Bailey.

"Even then, Liverpool were hanging on. They knew we'd given them a game and I remember their striker, Kenny Dalglish, taking a ball into the corner and just booting it into the crowd. They must have been worried."

If losing the League Cup to Liverpool dismayed Atkinson's men, it failed to destroy them. The manager would not allow it, not with another semi-final, in the FA Cup, against Arsenal on the horizon.

The teams met at Villa Park, Birmingham, on 16 April 1983. A crowd of 46,535 witnessed Tony Woodcock give Arsenal the lead before half-time. United's season of promise was on a precipice; the FA Cup was their last chance of silverware. They needed strong men to turn it around, and they found them in Robson, who levelled the scores, and Whiteside, who netted a wonderful winner on the volley.

So eight weeks after losing to Liverpool, Ron Atkinson led his team out at Wembley again,

this time against Brighton and Hove Albion.

Brighton were the biggest FA Cup final underdogs since 1976, when Southampton had shocked United, but Gordon Smith headed them into the lead on 14 minutes. United regained control of possession though and deservedly equalised on 55 minutes when a far-post cross by Mike Duxbury was lashed into the net by Frank Stapleton. Ray Wilkins curled in one of Wembley's all-time classic goals with his left foot on 74 minutes and the game seemed won. But with just three minutes remaining and red and white ribbon about to be tied to the trophy, Gary Stevens grabbed an equaliser, reviving memories of United's 1979 FA Cup final nightmare.

It looked like it was about to get even worse in the last minute of extra-time as Smith was left with just United keeper Gary Bailey to beat. "And Smith must score…" shouted the TV commentator. Instead, Bailey saved the ball using a combination of his legs and backside.

"That save probably won the cup for us, because if Smith's shot had gone in, I don't

August 1982
Cultured Dutch midfielder Arnold Muhren is signed from Ipswich Town.

October 1982
Ray Wilkins suffers a fractured cheekbone and loses the captaincy of both club and country to Bryan Robson.

March 1983
United lose the League Cup final 2–1 against Liverpool. Norman Whiteside becomes the youngest player ever to score in a League Cup final, aged 17 years and 323 days.

MANCHESTER UNITED **OFFICIAL MEMBERS' HISTORY BOOK** 99

Jubilant United players celebrate the
1983 FA Cup final replay win over Brighton.

think there would have been time to kick off," said defender Arthur Albiston later.

That save was the turning point. United destroyed Brighton 4–0 in the replay the following Thursday night at Wembley with goals from Robson (two), Whiteside and Muhren (penalty).

By winning a major trophy in his second season, Atkinson had whetted the fans' appetite for his third. But the start of the campaign was hampered by another major injury problem. England winger Steve Coppell, a United fans' favourite, had sustained a serious knee injury while on international duty. The damage proved irreparable and sadly Coppell's playing career came to a premature end at the age of 28.

Needing a new No. 11, Atkinson overlooked Alan Davies – who had replaced Coppell for the FA Cup final and replay – in favour of Arthur Graham, signed for £45,000 from Leeds United. Graham was a first-team regular for one season only.

The 1983/84 campaign produced some high-scoring victories, but also some of the lowest points of the Atkinson era. Just before

Christmas, Atkinson's old club Oxford embarrassed him in the League Cup, knocking United out over two legs. But Ron's face turned an even deeper shade of red in the new year, when his FA Cup holders slipped up on the south coast, losing 2–0 to Third Division side AFC Bournemouth.

As the nation laughed, the United players licked their wounds. After being humbled by Bournemouth, it seemed they would be on a hiding to nothing against mighty Barcelona, their quarter-final opponents in the Cup Winners' Cup.

The Barcelona squad boasted two international strikers in Diego Maradona and Bernd Schuster, while Atkinson's team were still novices in Europe by comparison. United had been knocked out of the UEFA Cup in 1982/83 by Valencia, and slender victories over Dukla Prague and Spartak Varna in the early rounds of 1983/84 had barely enhanced their European status.

The first leg, away at the Nou Camp, followed the form guide. The home team won 2–0 and flew to England a fortnight later, confident they would finish off United in Manchester. Man for

April 1983
United beat Arsenal 2–1 at Villa Park in the 1983 FA Cup semi-final. Earlier in the season, the Reds had also beaten Arsenal in the League Cup semi-final.

May 1983
United thrash Brighton 4–0 in the FA Cup final replay. Norman Whiteside becomes the youngest player ever to score in an FA Cup final, aged 18 years and 18 days.

October 1983
Promising young striker Mark Hughes comes on as substitute in a League Cup tie against Port Vale, his first game in the senior team.

man, Ron Atkinson's Reds were clearly the underdogs. But backed by some incredible support inside Old Trafford, United found the courage and quality of finishing not only to draw level, but to win the tie 3–2 on aggregate with two goals from Bryan Robson and one from Frank Stapleton.

"The atmosphere that night was the best I ever experienced at Old Trafford," says Albiston. "It wasn't just the Stretford End or United Road or the Scoreboard End, all the stands were bouncing. They gave us such a lift, it was like having two extra men in the team."

If that momentous cup match showed the feats which Ron Atkinson's United could achieve, the very next fixture demonstrated their major flaw – lack of consistency. 10 days after beating Barcelona, the Reds lost to West Bromwich Albion. The final Ten matches, starting with the Albion result, produced two wins, four draws and four defeats as injuries and Jekyll and Hyde form took its toll.

The European adventure ended in something of an anti-climax in the semi-final against Juventus. The damage was done in the first leg at Old Trafford. Juventus frustrated the injury-hit Reds, who were missing Muhren, Robson and Wilkins, and held them 1–1. A 1–2 defeat in the return at the Stadio Comunale confirmed United's fate.

Finishing fourth in the league, United had to be content with a place in the UEFA Cup the following season. Access to the Continent's premier tournament, the European Cup, was then exclusively for the winners of the previous year's competition and the champions of each country. United's bitter rivals Liverpool accomplished both criteria in 1984. They won the league and the European Cup and also, just for good measure, the League Cup.

United had been pioneers of the European Cup, the first English team to enter it in 1956, and the first English side to win it in 1968. But now the Reds of Manchester were trailing 4–1 to the Reds of Merseyside in terms of European Cup successes, and there was an even greater deficit in league championships – Liverpool 15, Manchester United 7.

Atkinson sensed he needed some big signings to close the gap, hence his triple plunge into the transfer market during the summer of 1984.

Danish winger Jesper Olsen was imported from Amsterdam, where he'd been one of the stars of another great Ajax team. Scotland striker Alan Brazil was bought from Tottenham. He had previously been one of Ipswich Town's heroes in the period when they won the FA Cup, UEFA Cup and twice finished second in the league. The third and final acquisition was Gordon Strachan from Aberdeen. He replaced Ray Wilkins who had joined AC Milan in June.

Both Strachan and Olsen had experienced winning a league championship, in Scotland and Holland respectively. No one else in the United dressing-room had such experience.

The new trio were all in the starting line-up

SHARP
Gordon Strachan

as the 1984/85 season kicked off, but although Strachan scored on his debut against Watford, United could not muster a victory in their first four league matches. Old Trafford witnessed 1–1 draws with Watford and Chelsea, while the same scoreline was recorded away at Ipswich Town. Even less inspiring was the 0–0 stalemate at Southampton.

United fans couldn't help but look enviously at Liverpool, who had the prolific Ian Rush in their armoury. All the Reds could hope for was a revival of the club's longstanding tradition of goal-sharing, and it duly came during a fruitful September. In the space of seven days, six different players scored for United against Newcastle United (5–0) and Coventry City (3–0). Opposing defenders just didn't know

December 1983
Ron Atkinson's old club Oxford beat United 2–1 in a League Cup replay at the Manor Ground.

January 1984
Media mogul Robert Maxwell tries and fails to take over United. On the pitch, Third Division AFC Bournemouth knock United out of the FA Cup, winning 2–0 at Dean Court.

March 1984
United come back from a 2–0 first leg deficit to beat mighty Barcelona 3–0 in the second leg at Old Trafford to qualify for the semi-final of the European Cup Winners' Cup.

MANCHESTER UNITED **OFFICIAL MEMBERS' HISTORY BOOK**   **101**

Powerhouse striker Mark Hughes broke into the first team in October 1983.

who to mark as the shots rained in from Moses, Olsen, Hughes, Robson, Strachan (twice) and Whiteside (twice).

United faced Rush in their very next fixture at Old Trafford. Not for the first or last time during Atkinson's reign, Arthur Albiston and his fellow defenders prevented the Liverpool striker from scoring and matched the champions. The final score was 1–1, with Strachan on the scoresheet for United.

"Liverpool were obviously the dominant team of that period," says Albiston. "But we knew we could beat them on the day.

"Just before the Big Ron era, Joe Jordan used to cause them all sorts of problems. He'd put his head in where some people wouldn't even dream of kicking the ball and that seemed to disrupt Liverpool. Mark Hughes and Norman Whiteside gave the best of defences a similarly hard time and that's why we got results against them."

It was against some of the smaller teams that United failed to deliver. During the 1984/85

league season, they lost to Stoke City, Sheffield Wednesday, Coventry City and Luton Town. Finishing fourth, they were again forced to mine the cup competitions for silverware.

In the UEFA Cup, for example, they knocked out Raba Gyor Eto from Hungary, the Dutch side PSV Eindhoven and, from north of the border, Dundee United. But just when United seemed on course for their first European final in 17 years, they were bounced out with two rounds to go.

Videoton, their curiously named quarter-final opponents from Budapest, had restricted the Reds to just one goal, scored by Stapleton, at Old Trafford. The Hungarians then won 1–0 on their quagmire of a pitch to send the tie into extra-time and finally a penalty shoot-out. Goalkeeper Peter Disztl crucially saved the sudden-death kick by Hughes. United kicked themselves; it was a tie they should have won comfortably.

At least United were compensated by their FA Cup run in 1985, despite a third-round draw which reminded them of their premature exit in the previous season. This time, with Bournemouth coming to Old Trafford, there was no repeat shock. Instead, goals by McQueen, Strachan and Stapleton buried the Cherries 3–0.

Next out of the FA Cup hat were Coventry City, fresh from winning 1–0 on United's turf in the league. That surprise result gave the Sky Blues plenty of confidence and made the fourth-round tie a tough one to call – that is until Mark Hughes and Paul McGrath scored for the Reds in their 2–1 triumph.

Reaching the fifth round of the FA Cup was just what the doctor ordered for Ron Atkinson, especially after medical reports had ruled out Bryan Robson for a few months with a dislocated shoulder. United fans knew the loss of the captain would be detrimental to the team's chances of success in the weekly rigours of league football, but round by round in the Cup, a solution could be found. McGrath seemed to be the answer, especially when he scored again in the 2–0 victory at Blackburn in

April 1984
Despite a valiant effort, United lose 3–2 on aggregate to Juventus in the European Cup Winners Cup semi-final.

May 1984
United finish fourth in the league, after drawing four, losing four and winning just two of their last 10 games.

June 1984
Ray Wilkins is sold to AC Milan. In summer, Atkinson also buys Gordon Strachan from Aberdeen, Jesper Olsen from Ajax and Alan Brazil from Spurs.

the fifth round.

In fact, the versatile Irishman could play in a number of positions. In the quarter-final against West Ham, he resumed his customary role at the heart of defence, following an injury to Kevin Moran.

Further forward, Atkinson shuffled his pack and proceeded to play Whiteside, Stapleton and Hughes in the same attacking side. The tactic worked a treat, as the Reds turned West Ham over 4–2 at Old Trafford with a second goal in the FA Cup run for Hughes adding to Whiteside's tremendous hat-trick.

For the people of Merseyside, the semi-final draw kept alive their dream of the perfect final – Liverpool versus Everton at Wembley Stadium. For United, drawn against Liverpool, it was the opportunity to spoil that dream and remind a few people that Manchester was still a football city to be reckoned with.

Everton's Goodison Park was selected as the neutral venue. United had just beaten Liverpool 1–0 in the league at Anfield, thanks to a strike by Stapleton.

Big Frank struck again in the semi-final in extra-time, after Ronnie Whelan had cancelled out the opening goal by Hughes. United were leading 2–1 in the 120th minute of the match when Paul Walsh, seemingly from an offside position, levelled again for Liverpool to make the final score 2–2.

Everton, in the meantime, had won through to the final. They waited patiently as United and Liverpool squared up again in the replay, this time at Maine Road.

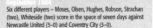
Arthur Albiston

After twice being behind in the first match, Liverpool took the lead in the second game when Paul McGrath inadvertently headed the ball past his own goalkeeper, Gary Bailey.

The all-Merseyside final looked odds-on at half-time in the replay, but Bryan Robson, back from injury, had other ideas. The Manchester United midfielder equalized with one of the

greatest goals of his career, a long-range drive into the top corner of Bruce Grobbelaar's net. Then as captain, he cajoled his colleagues into completing their comeback with another marvellous finish by Mark Hughes.

United had reached their fifth FA Cup final in 10 seasons, and the third Wembley final of Ron Atkinson's reign.

Eight years after wrecking Liverpool's tilt at the treble, Manchester United were ready to ruin the dream season of Everton, who had already won the 1985 league championship and European Cup Winners' Cup.

Arthur Albiston, an FA Cup-winner in 1977 and 1983, knew it wouldn't be an easy match. After all, Everton had thrashed United 5–0 during the season and had knocked them out of the League Cup. They had also won two trophies and boasted a well-balanced midfield.

"They had two wide men, Trevor Steven on the right and Kevin Sheedy on the left, with two hard-working players in the middle, Paul Bracewell and Peter Reid," remembers Albiston. "They weren't the tallest of players, but they were very determined and they did a lot of defensive work."

In a bid to break down what effectively was an eight-man defence, Ron Atkinson selected an attacking team, including former striker Norman Whiteside in midfield.

Between the two teams there was enough talent to thrill Wembley's capacity crowd of 100,000, not to mention the millions watching on television. Yet they managed to cancel each other out and produce more than 90 minutes of stalemate, as the rigours of a long season affected both sets of players.

Socks were already low down shattered legs when the crowd was stirred from its slumbers by the first major incident. Kevin Moran's controversial sending off, the first in an FA Cup final, brought the game to life and forced United to reshuffle for the last 12 minutes of

September 1984
Six different players – Moses, Olsen, Hughes, Robson, Strachan (two), Whiteside (two) score in the space of seven days against Newcastle United (5–0) and Coventry City (3–0).

January 1985
Bryan Robson suffers a dislocated shoulder, affecting both United and England with the 1986 World Cup approaching.

March 1985
Hungarian team Videoton beat United on penalties in the UEFA Cup quarter-finals after the two-leg tie finishes 1–1 on aggregate.

normal time, then extra time. Moran was dismissed for a mis-timed tackle on Peter Reid, and Frank Stapleton replaced him as an emergency centre-half.

United battled on with 10 men, and finally made the breakthrough in the 110th minute of the match.

"Gordon Strachan deserves a pat on the back," recalls Albiston, "because he ran 40 or 50 yards, overlapped Norman and distracted Van den Hauwe and Ratcliffe. Norman then cut inside and scored a wonderful goal.

"I had been substituted by then, so I was sat on the bench, directly behind Norman and as soon as he took it inside on his left foot, I could see the goal coming. He hit the exact spot where Neville Southall had put his spare gloves, right in the corner of the net. I'd injured my ankle, kicking Peter Reid, but somehow I managed to leap in the air and jump on top of Ron."

It was an extraordinary goal to win a very ordinary match. Yet another contradiction in the life of United in the Eighties.

United also fared very well at the start of the following league season, 1985/86, winning their first 10 matches in a row. It was a remarkable run, not least because the team scored so many goals, 27, and conceded so few, three.

With maximum league points gained from the first 10 games, it seemed that United would never be in a better position to go on and win the league championship. After all, none of the great sides at Liverpool had ever made such a perfect start to a season. But Ron Atkinson believes his team were closer to the title in 1983/84, when they were ahead of Liverpool with only 10 games left to play. Then an injury to Robson had ruined United's chances and he was absent again in 1985 when the team's 10-point lead disappeared. United won just four of the next 10 games and lost at Sheffield Wednesday and Leicester City in the

process. By the end of the calendar year, they had suffered two more defeats, back to back against Arsenal at Old Trafford and away to the league champions Everton on Boxing Day. They had also been knocked out of the League Cup, at Anfield of all places. Unluckily for Atkinson, it was the 13th time his United side had faced Liverpool, and yet it was only their third defeat.

Arthur Albiston remembers the Reds were still in contention for the title until March: "Then we just seemed to crack up, with the same old mix of injuries to key players and poor displays."

The poor form in March ended United's run in the FA Cup. After drawing 1–1 at West Ham in the fifth round, they lost the replay 2–0 at Old Trafford. By May, the Reds were in no position to prevent their great rivals Liverpool from achieving their greatest feat so far – the league and FA Cup double.

After all they had promised with their opening run, United again finished fourth in the First Division, with exactly the same record of results as the previous year – played 42, won 22, drawn 10, lost 10.

Paul McGrath

The captain and star player, Bryan Robson, had played half of those fixtures but it wasn't just his No. 7 shirt that had been passed around the squad. Keeper Gary Bailey lost his No. 1 jersey through injury and was replaced by Chris Turner from February onwards. The central defensive pairing went through several permutations, from Graeme Hogg and McGrath to Moran and Billy Garton. Even Arthur Albiston missed a few games in December, when Colin Gibson played at left-back.

"We didn't have the same strength in depth that the United teams in the late Nineties had," laments Albiston. "If we had two or three influential players out, we couldn't cope."

The televised 1986 World Cup finals provided more moments of anxiety in Ron

April 1985
United avert an all-Merseyside FA Cup final beating Liverpool 2–1 in a semi-final replay through goals from Robson and Hughes.

May 1985
United finish fourth in the league but go on to win the FA Cup final against Everton 1–0. Kevin Moran becomes the first man to be sent off in a Cup final.

September 1985
United have a dream start to the new season, winning every one of their first 10 games. A 1–1 draw away to Luton ends the sequence.

1985: Another FA Cup success for Big Ron's team.

Atkinson's living room. Several of his players were representing their countries in Mexico, and several of them returned home with injuries that would delay their starts to the new season. Bryan Robson, inevitably, was among the walking wounded. After dislocating his shoulder again on England duty, he missed United's first four games of 1986/87 – three straight defeats and a draw.

When Robson returned to the team, United returned to winning ways, but for one match only. Impressive though it was to beat Southampton 5–1, the euphoria was soon forgotten when the Reds lost their next three in a row, to Watford, Everton and Chelsea.

"We made an horrendous start," says Albiston, reflecting on the run of six defeats in eight games. "Teams that we would normally wipe the floor with could sense that we were not quite firing on all cylinders. I remember we lost at home to Charlton when they had only just been promoted. Again, you can harp on about certain players being injured, but even so, results like that shouldn't happen to a club of Manchester United's stature."

Atkinson was sinking. He had already given some thought to resigning in the summer but

had been persuaded to stay for at least one more season by his chairman, Martin Edwards. By the end of September, both parties must have been regretting that stay of execution. United were languishing in the lower half of the table, and although their league form in October showed some improvement, their next meeting with Southampton indicated otherwise.

Drawn out of the hat together in the League Cup, the sides drew 0–0 at Old Trafford and headed for a replay at the Dell. Future England star Matt Le Tissier destroyed United, who were again without their own national hero, Bryan Robson.

On the following morning, Wednesday 5 November, Atkinson finally became the fall guy. Later that day, while people across England celebrated Bonfire Night with firework displays, the sacked United manager reminisced about his five-year reign in the company of friends and a few of his now former players. Gordon Strachan, Bryan Robson and Norman Whiteside, all present at the farewell party, would now have to live up to their big reputations for a new man at the helm of Manchester United.

May 1986
United fade to a fourth-place finish in the league yet again. And Mark Hughes plays his last match before moving to Barcelona for £1.8 million.

September 1986
United make a terrible start to the 1986/87 season, losing six of their first eight league games.

November 1986
A 1–4 hammering by Southampton at the Dell marks the end of Ron Atkinson's managerial reign. A day later on Bonfire Night, he is sacked.

Seeking the right balance: Alex Ferguson's early years at United were spent laying the foundations for long-term success.

CHAPTER TWELVE

THE FERGUSON REVOLUTION

Success was elusive in the early years of Alex Ferguson's managerial reign, but his indomitable spirit and foresight in developing the club's youth system would yield rich rewards in the long-term…

Alex Ferguson, was brought up in the tough Govan district of Glasgow, and began his professional life as a toolmaker at the Clyde shipyards. Aged 19, he became a union leader, and showed he wasn't one for shirking big decisions by leading his fellow workers out on strike at one stage.

After a playing career as a centre-forward that took in Queen's Park, St Johnstone, Dunfermline, Rangers, Falkirk and Ayr United, he brought his determined approach to football management. After three months in charge of East Stirling, he went to St Mirren and transformed the club, leading them to the First Division title.

He moved on to Aberdeen where he broke the Celtic–Rangers stranglehold on Scottish football. Under his leadership, Aberdeen were crowned Scottish champions three times, they won the Scottish Cup four times (achieving the Double in 1984) and the Scottish League Cup once. They also triumphed in Europe, winning the Cup Winners' Cup in 1983.

It was an impressive record, and in 1986, following a sojourn as Scotland's caretaker manager at the Mexico World Cup, Ferguson was installed in the Old Trafford hot seat.

His early years in the job were an important period of transition for the club, affecting not only the public face of the first team but also the situation behind the scenes and at grassroots level.

English football's most successful odyssey started inauspiciously though. On 8 November 1986, Alex Ferguson lost his first fixture as Manchester United manager 2–0 against Oxford United at the Manor Ground.

He could really only take the team in one direction, and United finished the season 11th, higher than they were placed when he took charge.

The highlights of Ferguson's first six months at Old Trafford included a 2–0 victory over Arsenal, who would emerge as league champions within two years, home and away wins over defending champions Liverpool, a 4–1 thrashing of Newcastle United, and triumph in two Manchester derbies.

But the supporters had to swallow some disappointments, notably being knocked out of the FA Cup in the fourth round by Coventry City, the eventual winners of the competition.

The search for greater stability started in earnest during the summer of 1987, Ferguson's first close season as Manchester United manager. Frank Stapleton, Ron Atkinson's first signing, was sold to Ajax in July, and swiftly replaced by prolific striker Brian McClair, an £850,000 buy from Celtic. On the same day that McClair met the press at Old Trafford, England defender Viv Anderson was also unveiled as a new signing, arriving from Arsenal.

Both players settled in very well at Old

TIMELINE

November 1986
On 7 November 1986, Alex Ferguson is appointed the manager of Manchester United.

January 1987
United lose to Coventry City 1–0 at home in the FA Cup fourth round.

April 1987
Ferguson's United complete a league double over Liverpool, beating them 1–0 at Old Trafford, but the Reds would finish the season in 11th place.

MANCHESTER UNITED **OFFICIAL MEMBERS' HISTORY BOOK**   **107**

Brian McClair was Alex Ferguson's first signing alongside Viv Anderson.

Trafford and helped the evolving team to second place in 1987/88, the club's highest league finish since 1979/80. United finished just nine points behind one of the greatest Liverpool teams in history.

Brian McClair scored 24 First Division goals, making him the first United player since George Best to net more than 20 in one league season, but he admits United were never in touching distance of Liverpool:

"We had a fantastic run towards the end of the season, when we were unbeaten for three months, but we were playing for second place from Christmas because they were flying."

That defender Steve Bruce signed from Norwich (for £800,000) in December 1987, and United enjoyed a strong finish to the season was no coincidence. Bruce, 27, lacked pace and had been rejected by numerous clubs in his teenage years, but his organisational skills, ability to read the game and encouragement of young players would prove a huge asset in years to come.

The Reds finished Ferguson's first full season empty-handed though. Their League Cup run had ended where the new manager's United career had started, in defeat at Oxford's Manor Ground (2–0). Being knocked out of the FA Cup at Highbury (2–1) was another bitter pill to swallow, especially when Arsenal defender Nigel Winterburn barracked Brian McClair for missing a spot-kick that would have levelled the scores.

In summer 1988, Alex Ferguson signed his former Aberdeen goalkeeper Jim Leighton and the club's returning prodigal son, Mark Hughes, as he aimed to close the gap on Liverpool. But the Reds started the 1988/89 season very poorly. At one stage they went through nine games without a win, a sequence that seemed to stem from United's inability to kill off teams. In eight of those matches, they took the lead only to let it slip again, often in the last 20 minutes.

After an awful autumn, the Reds enjoyed a merry Christmas, beating Nottingham Forest 2–0 on Boxing Day and Liverpool 3–1 on New Year's Day. In the match against the champions, all four goals were scored between the 70th minute, when John Barnes gave Liverpool the lead, and the 77th minute when Russell Beardsmore capped United's amazing, instant comeback.

It was a big day for Beardsmore and the other young players in Alex Ferguson's team, namely the two Lees at right-back and left-back, Martin and Sharpe, and the substitute striker Mark Robins who was called into action in the first half following an injury to Gordon Strachan.

Martin, Beardsmore, Sharpe, Robins and the goalkeeper Gary Walsh were the leading lights of a larger group which also included Derek Brazil, Tony Gill, Deiniol Graham, Giuliano Maiorana and David Wilson. Collectively, they were known in the media as 'Fergie's Fledglings'. But while their emergence demonstrated Alex's faith in young talent, the fact they had to play in so many games showed how badly the senior ranks were hit

TIMELINE

July 1987
Ferguson's first signings are Celtic striker Brian McClair and Arsenal defender Viv Anderson.

December 1987
Central defender Steve Bruce is signed from Norwich for £800,000.

April 1988
Brian McClair scores his 20th league goal of the season in the 3–0 home win against Luton Town, the first player to do so since George Best, 20 years earlier.

108 MANCHESTER UNITED OFFICIAL MEMBERS' HISTORY BOOK

by injury. The defence, in particular, was badly affected with first-choice full-backs Viv Anderson and Colin Gibson starting just seven games between them in 1988/89, while central stalwart Paul McGrath missed almost half of that season's fixtures.

Alex Ferguson wondered in hindsight if he'd been a bit hasty in releasing so many senior players, especially the defenders Arthur Albiston, Graeme Hogg and Kevin Moran, who all left the club before the 1987/88 season started. They were later followed through the exit gates by striker Peter Davenport and the midfielders Liam O'Brien, Jesper Olsen and, in the most unpopular departure of all, Gordon Strachan. The latter was sold to Leeds in March 1989, just two days after playing for United in the FA Cup quarter-final at Old Trafford. The Reds were controversially knocked out 1–0 by Nottingham Forest – the referee, Brian Hill, decided what looked a certain goal for United did not cross the line.

The manner of that defeat and the subsequent sale of Strachan sent United spinning into decline. They won two of their last 11 matches, losing seven, and finished in 11th place. Arsenal won the title, pipping Liverpool on goal difference.

Paul McGrath was shown the door in August 1989, sold to Aston Villa for a bargain £450,000 fee. McGrath was a central figure in the drinking culture Ferguson had inherited, and he finally lost patience with this hugely talented but woefully indisciplined player.

Michael
Knighton

The time for Alex Ferguson to spend some serious money had arrived. By the end of September 1989, he had splashed out more than £7 million on players, starting with midfielders Mike Phelan from Norwich City and Neil Webb from Nottingham Forest. Both made their debuts on the opening day of the season and they were briefly joined on the field by the wealthy tycoon Michael Knighton,

the apparent new owner of Manchester United. He introduced himself to the fans by juggling with the ball. But like the team, the businessman flattered to deceive. After the euphoria of that opening 4–1 win over Arsenal, life soon returned to normal. Knighton's takeover deal fell through and the Reds again fell from grace, losing four of their next six league games.

By far the worst result of that sequence and season was the 5–1 defeat by Manchester City on 23 September 1989.

"That was hard because you couldn't just sit in the house and hide," recalls Brian McClair. "I knew people who were City fans, but we just had to take the medicine and get on with it. It was a lesson for all of us."

United were in mourning, not only for the dramatic loss of their supremacy in Manchester but also for the premature death of their championship chances. The midfield dream team of Phelan, Robson and Webb had already been wiped out by a serious injury to the latter, while the other new signings Paul Ince, Gary Pallister and Danny Wallace were struggling to settle in.

Gary Pallister in particular was under the greatest scrutiny, having been signed from Middlesbrough for a British record fee of £2.3 million. Alex Ferguson needed a settled partnership in central defence, and he was hoping that Pallister would form exactly that with Steve Bruce.

United finished the 1989/90 season in 13th place, their lowest position since being relegated in 1974. Little wonder, then, that the players sought solace in the FA Cup.

"The Cup games were a relief because there was so much pressure on us to try and stay in the division," admits McClair. "We finished only six places off the bottom and there was a point when we were in real danger of going down. We hadn't won for 11 games and went

May 1988
A three-month unbeaten run culminates in a second-place finish in the First Division. Ferguson signs keeper Jim Leighton from Aberdeen.

June 1988
Mark Hughes re-signs for United after an unhappy spell at Barcelona.

January 1989
Fergie's first batch of fledglings break through, including 17-year old Lee Sharpe and Russell Beardsmore, who scores in a 3–1 New Years Day win over Liverpool.

MANCHESTER UNITED **OFFICIAL MEMBERS' HISTORY BOOK**   **109**

Lee Martin smashes home the winner in the 1990 FA Cup final replay against Crystal Palace.

to Millwall (10 February 1990) with only a few senior players; the rest were kids or reserves. It was never an easy place to go to but we won, and it turned us in the right direction."

Some observers still maintain that Ferguson would have been sacked had it not been for the face-saving FA Cup run, but Brian McClair, for one, isn't convinced by that argument:

"My view was that although the first team was struggling, the board were pleased with some of the other things that he'd sorted out, such as the youth set-up that later came to fruition. Somebody once said he was lucky, and I suppose at some point luck carried us through in the FA Cup that year."

The press vultures gathered at the City Ground in January 1990, hoping Nottingham Forest would knock Fergie's men out in the third round. But even with the likes of Ince, Robson and Webb injured and watching from the sidelines, United found the necessary steel and spirit to sneak through 1–0, with Mark Robins scoring the winner.

A Clayton Blackmore goal gave United another single-goal victory in the fourth round away to Hereford United, and the team were 'rewarded' with yet another away tie, against First Division side Newcastle United.

The live television cameras captured a classic, with the Magpies equalizing twice to keep the game on a knife-edge. Brian McClair then netted the winner (to clinch a 3–2 win), a feat he repeated against the Blades of Sheffield United in round six in a cagey 1–0 win.

The semi-final clash with Oldham Athletic was played at Maine Road and had all the characteristics of a passionate local derby. The blue-shirted Latics drew first blood when Earl Barrett fired them into an early lead. United's midfield duo of Robson and Webb had recovered from injury in time to play in the match, and after captain Robson equalized in the 29th minute, his partner put the Reds 2–1 up with less than 20 minutes to go. Agonisingly, Oldham striker Ian Marshall equalized to force extra-time.

The fatigue factor challenged both teams, but both Joe Royle and Alex Ferguson had utilized their substitutes wisely. The two number 12s, Wallace for United and Palmer for Oldham, both scored in extra time to ensure honours remained even.

After the 3–3 thriller, the teams returned to Maine Road for the replay three days later. This time, the scoring was comparatively sparse, McClair's goal after 50 minutes seemingly

March 1989
Ferguson sells popular midfielder Gordon Strachan to Leeds United.

May 1989
Following Strachan's departure, United spiral into decline, winning just two of their last 11 games to finish in 11th place in the league.

August 1989
Businessman Michael Knighton apparently is set to take over the club, but the deal eventually falls through. Defender Gary Pallister joins United from Middlesbrough for a record £2.3 million fee.

sufficient for United to advance to Wembley for the first time during Ferguson's reign. But then, with nine minutes to go, former Old Trafford favourite, Andy Ritchie, popped up to force extra-time again.

The stage was set for Mark Robins to become the FA Cup hero once again. Brought on as a substitute, he scored to win the tie for United, just as he had done in the third round.

The first FA Cup final of Alex Ferguson's reign against Crystal Palace revived memories of the corresponding fixture in Ron Atkinson's career in 1983. Like Brighton, Crystal Palace had beaten Liverpool on their way to Wembley (in the semi-final) but they were still considered the underdogs.

Sadly for United, the echoes of '83 didn't end there. Palace (managed by United old boy Steve Coppell) scored the first goal in the 18th minute, a mere four minutes later than Brighton had done. Fortunately, the Reds equalized far quicker this time around when Robson headed the ball past Nigel Martyn in the 35th minute. The United captain closed in on his record third FA Cup triumph in the second half when Mark Hughes scored.

The tide turned again when Coppell sent on Ian Wright. The live-wire substitute scored just three minutes after making his entrance, and then again just inside extra-time.

"At that point, 3–2 down with not long left in the match, some of us were thinking it's not going to be our year, we're not going to make it," admits Lee Martin, United's left-back. "But with eight minutes to go, Mark Hughes popped up to score the equalizer. It was a big relief, to be given an extra chance in the replay."

One goal-scoring chance in the replay was all Lee Martin needed to make history. The defender, who had only netted one goal for United, chested down a pass from Neil Webb and blasted the ball into the Wembley net, 59 minutes into an otherwise dull encounter.

While Martin made most of the headlines, he had to share some of the media glare with Jim Leighton. But the goalkeeper's story was not a happy one. After conceding three goals in the first match, Leighton was replaced for the replay by Les Sealey.

"Jim was a smashing bloke, but being dropped by the manager just destroyed him," says Lee Martin. "In fact, it was devastating for all of us because he was a friend of ours. Les offered to give him his medal, but he didn't take it."

Devastating as it was for Leighton, the decision showed Alex Ferguson's ruthless pragmatism and willingness to put the club's interests above personal ties.

Manchester United were on the march again and a return to European competition beckoned in 1990/91.

The five-year European ban on all English clubs following the Heysel Stadium tragedy had been a source of frustration for Ferguson and his players, especially in 1988, when they would have qualified for the UEFA Cup as league runners-up. That frustration was unleashed on Hungarian team Pecsi Munkas, United's opponents in the first round of the European Cup Winners' Cup, who were easily despatched 3–0 on aggregate.

Brian McClair had scored in Hungary, and he was on the scoresheet again in the following round, at home to Wrexham. The Welsh Cup-holders were to finish the season

Lee Martin savours FA Cup success with his team-mates.

January 1990
Under-fire manager Ferguson is given some breathing space as a Mark Robins goal clinches an FA Cup third round victory over Nottingham Forest.

May 1990
United finish a lowly thirteenth in the league, but a 1–0 final replay win over Crystal Palace secures the FA Cup.

June 1990
Full-back Denis Irwin is signed from Oldham Athletic for £625,000.

MANCHESTER UNITED **OFFICIAL MEMBERS' HISTORY BOOK**   **111**

at the bottom of the entire Football League, but they put up a brave fight before finally surrendering to United 5–0 on aggregate.

Victory over Wrexham booked a place in the quarter-finals, to be played in March 1991. But that wasn't the only thing Reds fans could look forward to as they welcomed in the new year. The team was through to the last eight of the League Cup, having knocked out the two sides who were vying for the title. Beating the champions Liverpool 3–1 in the fourth round was impressive enough, but United achieved an even greater victory in the fifth round. United thrashed Arsenal 6–2 at Highbury, with goals from Blackmore, Hughes, Wallace and a fantastic hat-trick by Lee Sharpe.

"We battered Arsenal, when nobody had given us a chance," recalls Brian McClair. "It was a phenomenal game, but we needed to be capable of doing that week in, week out. The disappointing thing was that we still weren't."

Hence United's final league position of sixth, where they were sandwiched between Manchester City and Wimbledon. The one point deducted by the FA for a mass brawl with Arsenal at Old Trafford had no bearing on this, and the Gunners still won the championship, despite losing two points for the regrettable incident.

With no chance of challenging for the title, and their FA Cup campaign cut short in the fifth round by Norwich, United's hopes of winning domestic honours in 1990/91 rested with the Rumbelows Cup. After beating Leeds United in both legs of the semi-final (2–1 at Old Trafford, 1–0 at Elland Road), the Reds were hot favourites to beat another Yorkshire team in the final. Instead, the underdogs of Sheffield Wednesday won the Cup, thanks to a goal by Manchester-born John Sheridan, and the guidance of ex-United boss Ron Atkinson.

There was little time to dwell on the Wembley defeat because three days later the Reds had to face Legia Warsaw in the second leg of the Cup Winners' Cup semi-final. United had won the first leg in Poland 3–1, the same score by which they had beaten Montpellier over two legs in the quarter-final.

Lee Sharpe gave the Reds a good start to the second leg against Legia when he made the aggregate score 4–1, and even though the Poles forced a draw on the night at Old Trafford, United were not to be denied their place in another final.

Alex Ferguson had tasted some success in Europe, winning the Cup-Winners' Cup with Aberdeen in 1983 against all the odds. His opponents then had been the mighty Real Madrid, so it was something of a coincidence that another Spanish side, Barcelona, blocked his path to glory with Manchester United. His opposite number in May 1991, Johan Cruyff, was a master tactician, so the build-up to the final became a battle of wits.

Fergie, for example, elected to counter the ball-playing abilities of Barcelona's best player, Ronald Koeman. Like his manager Cruyff, the Dutch defender was on home soil in Rotterdam, but he was unable to influence the game as he would have liked with Brian McClair detailed to close him down. Mark Hughes' mission was to destroy his former club and prove his Spanish critics wrong.

With a settled back four of Irwin, Bruce, Pallister and Blackmore protected by Ince and Robson in midfield, United were in no mood to be broken down by Barcelona and neither side gave anything away in a cagey first half.

When the tempo picked up in the second half, United were in their element. In the 67th minute, Hughes was fouled outside the area by Alexanco, one of his former team-mates. Robson put the ball down and launched his free kick towards the far post, where Bruce sent it towards goal with a towering header and Hughes applied the finish. 1–0.

Lee Sharpe

November 1990
United destroy Arsenal 6–2 in a League Cup tie at Highbury, with Lee Sharpe grabbing a brilliant hat-trick.

April 1991
United are beaten 1–0 by Sheffield Wednesday in the League Cup final. Manchester-born John Sheridan scores the winner for Wednesday.

May 1991
Ryan Giggs makes his full United debut against Manchester City. And on 15 May, United beat Barcelona 2–1 in the European Cup Winners' Cup final in Rotterdam, thus securing United's first European trophy for 23 years.

Sensing that their opponents were on the ropes, United pressed forward in search of a second goal. On 72 minutes, 'Sparky' Hughes delivered the crucial strike. This time he had to shoot from what looked like an impossible angle, having run the ball wide to the goalkeeper's left from Robson's precise pass. For the second time in 12 months, Hughes had scored two goals in a cup final.

Koeman caused anxiety for the 25,000 expectant United fans inside the Feyenoord Stadium in Rotterdam when he made the score 2–1, but Clayton Blackmore prevented calamity when he cleared Michael Laudrup's shot off the line. That narrow escape ended Barcelona's hopes of an equalizer, and completed a momentous win for the men from Manchester.

Having won the club's first European trophy for 23 years, Alex Ferguson's United seemed to be ready to make a strong challenge for the championship, which had been absent from Old Trafford for an even longer period. The manager himself stuck his neck out and told the press his Reds were ripe for the title race.

Fergie's optimism seemed well-founded when his summer signings, Peter Schmeichel and Paul Parker, galvanized the defence to such an extent that United started the season with four consecutive clean sheets. They joined Bruce, Pallister and Denis Irwin, who had been signed from Oldham in 1990, in a formidable back five.

With his shock of blond hair and imposing six-foot-four-inch frame, Danish international goalkeeper Peter Schmeichel really looked the part. Voted the Danish Player of the Year, his transfer fee of £500,000 from IF Brondby was a snip – indeed, Alex Ferguson would later reflect: "I believe we made the buy of the century."

The manager also found fresh impetus for the attack, deploying Andrei Kanchelskis, on the right wing and an emerging youngster named Ryan Giggs on the left.

Since the heyday of George Best, United fans had waited in vain for a player with similar God-given talent, and at last, in Giggs they found him. A Welshman raised in Manchester, Giggs was a product of United's burgeoning youth system. He'd made his first-team debut aged 17 as a sub against Everton late on in the 1990/91 season, and an injury to Lee Sharpe early in 1991/92 gave him the chance to

August 1991
United sign Danish international goalkeeper Peter Schmeichel from IF Brondby for £500,000.

September 1991
United beat Luton Town 5–0 at Old Trafford to make it seven clean sheets in their first nine league games.

October 1991
United complete a 4–1 aggregate win over Cambridge United in the opening round of the League Cup.

MANCHESTER UNITED **OFFICIAL MEMBERS' HISTORY BOOK**   113

establish himself. It was immediately apparent that the whippet-thin winger could cut it at the highest level – his innate sense of balance and ability to run with the ball at lightning speed made him a defender's worst nightmare.

Giggs' achievements in his first full season were extraordinary: he became the youngest-ever Welsh international (aged 17 years and 321 days), was crowned the PFA Young Player of the Year and also captained United's youth team to victory in the FA Youth Cup.

The new-look team enjoyed an excellent first half to 1991/92, tempered only by their exit from the Cup-Winners' Cup at the hands of Atletico Madrid. There was some degree of compensation for the Reds in the form of the European Super Cup, which they won 1–0 at Old Trafford in November 1991. Brian McClair scored the winning goal against the European champions, Red Star Belgrade.

Prior to New Year's Day, United lost just one league match, 3–2 to Sheffield Wednesday. Even then United were unlucky to lose the game, their 13th of the season, after leading 2–1 through McClair's two goals. The points

were almost in the bag when substitute Nigel Jemson also scored twice, late in the day.

The team's response to that blip was to win six of their next seven matches, admirably netting 20 goals in the process. McClair scored in four consecutive games, including a double on Boxing Day in the thrilling 6–3 victory at Oldham Athletic. It was a shame he couldn't make it five in a row, because the very next game was against Leeds United, Manchester United's rivals in the title race.

The two sides met three times in three different competitions between 29 December and 15 January, all at Elland Road. The Reds won the mini-series by some measure, knocking the Yorkshire club out of the FA Cup (1–0) and out of the Rumbelows Cup (3–1). But the one match against Leeds that Manchester United didn't win later proved to be the most important result. Had Alex Ferguson's team won 1–0, instead of drawing 1–1, they would have taken a seven-point lead in the league. But a late equalizer from the penalty spot perfectly summed up Leeds's resilience and which ultimately gave them the

Goalkeeping hero Les Sealey and Alex Ferguson celebrate United's 2–1 victory in the 1991 European Cup Winners Cup final.

November 1991
United win the European Super Cup, beating Red Star Belgrade 1–0 at Old Trafford. Brian McClair scores the winner.

December 1991
By the turn of the year, United have lost one league game, but a 1–1 draw at Elland Road on 29 December would later prove costly.

January 1992
United beat Leeds twice in a week, first in the League Cup (3–1) and then the FA Cup (1–0).

edge in the championship race.

"We would never take any credit away from Leeds because they stuck at it doggedly all year," says McClair. "But it was interesting that the change in the back-pass law killed them the following year. We were the more exciting team, trying to steamroller the opposition."

The high-tempo, all-guns-blazing approach eventually took its toll on United's title challenge, not least because they were forced to play their last six league matches in 17 days. In some ways they were victims of their own success, the problem of fixture congestion partly caused by their run in the Rumbelows Cup. This culminated in the Reds winning the competition for the very first time.

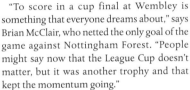

Ryan Giggs

"To score in a cup final at Wembley is something that everyone dreams about," says Brian McClair, who netted the only goal of the game against Nottingham Forest. "People might say now that the League Cup doesn't matter, but it was another trophy and that kept the momentum going."

Unfortunately United's momentum in the 1991/92 title race did not continue for much longer. The final furlong started well enough, with a home win over Southampton followed by an away draw at Luton. But then one or two tired players, perhaps understandably, took their foot off the pedal and the Reds paid dearly for it.

"We lost it because we had to play so many games towards the end of the season," reflects Brian. "We lost at home to Forest at Easter when Giggsy and Sharpey decided to go to Blackpool for the night. Then we just couldn't win a game. We had nothing left."

Two days after the 2–1 defeat by Forest on Easter Monday, the Reds were beaten 1–0 by West Ham in midweek and then at the end of a miserable seven days, they finally surrendered the title in the most painful manner. Their bitter 2–0 defeat by Liverpool on Sunday 26

April handed the championship to Leeds, who had won their match at Sheffield United earlier that day. The teams still had one fixture left to play and United won theirs, 3–1 against Tottenham, but this was an irrelevance after the agony of losing at Anfield.

"We had to sit there all summer thinking about what a nightmare it had been," remembers McClair. "People said we'd bottled it. In fact, it just gave us more of an identity as a team, and made us more determined to ensure it would never happen again. When we returned for pre-season, the gaffer put to us the same question he asks every year, 'Are you willing to climb back to the top of the mountain?' And we were. We were willing and ready."

With Ferguson's United revolution nearing completion, professional football in general was being revamped radically. In summer, Manchester United removed another of the old bastions of the English game – terracing – as recommended by the Taylor Report on the Hillsborough tragedy. It meant demolishing the famous Stretford End, and starting work on a new stand costing £10 million and containing 10,164 seats, with the major changes due to be completed during the 1992–93 season. It was the start of a process that would eventually see the capacity of all-seater Old Trafford become 67,700.

In 1992/93, United would be compete in the inaugural FA Premier League. Led by the satellite broadcasting company BSkyB, television raised the profile of the game and began to exert an influence over how it looked and when it would be played. Names on shirts, massive wage hikes, fireworks, dancing girls, Monday night matches and an influx of foreign players were just a few features of the new face of English football. At United, the imminent arrival of one particular foreign player was about to make all the difference.

March 1992
Two consecutive goalless draws against Wimbledon and Queen's Park Rangers hit United's league title hopes.

April 1992
United beat Nottingham Forest 1–0 in the League Cup final, with Brian McClair scoring the crucial goal.

May 1992
Six games in the last 17 days of the season take their toll, and United are pipped to the league championship by Leeds United.

MANCHESTER UNITED **OFFICIAL MEMBERS' HISTORY BOOK** 115

Eric Cantona: the catalyst
for a new era of success.

CHAPTER THIRTEEN
OOH AAH
ERIC
CANTONA!

Manchester United fans had high hopes of a first league title success in 26 years when the 1992/93 season got underway. The team just needed that extra spark. On 27 November 1992, Eric Cantona signed…

Despite cup triumphs at home and in Europe, Alex Ferguson knew that his tenure as United manager would never be considered truly successful unless he achieved the ultimate domestic prize – the league championship. But after 26 years, six managers and several near-misses, it had been so many years coming that some fans despaired of ever seeing United reach the pinnacle again.

"Since Sir Matt Busby last won the championship, it had become an obsession in Manchester," admits former boss Tommy Docherty. "And the longer the wait, the harder it became for anyone at the club to win it. After coming so close before Leeds United pipped them to it, it became even more difficult."

As the 1992/93 season got under way, there were few signs that this would be the campaign to end the wait for glory. Before it had even begun, there was disappointment for supporters. England's most successful striker, Alan Shearer, snubbed United, joining Blackburn Rovers from Southampton, while popular forward Mark Robins was sold to Norwich City. The arrival at Old Trafford of Dion Dublin proved scant consolation when the former Cambridge striker broke his leg just three games into his United career.

Defeats by Sheffield United, Everton, Wimbledon and Aston Villa in the first third of the season compounded the mood of pessimism as the team slipped to 10th in the table. The lack of goal power didn't bode well. Something spectacular was needed to turn the tide. Fortunately, that something arrived with an unexpected signing.

On Thursday 26 November, the United chairman Martin Edwards received a call from Bill Fotherby, Leeds United's financial director. Fotherby wanted to know if Denis Irwin was for sale. Edwards forwarded the enquiry to Alex Ferguson, who replied in the negative. On a whim however – probably sparked by United's lack of consistency in front of goal – Ferguson asked if Leeds would consider selling Eric Cantona, their charismatic, if somewhat temperamental, striker. It was a cheeky request because Cantona was a cult figure with the Elland Road faithful. Unexpectedly, Leeds agreed to discuss the matter and the following day Cantona and Ferguson met at a Holiday Inn in Manchester. An hour and a half later, Cantona was a Manchester United player.

Ironically, the best £1.2 million ever spent in the history of the transfer market was initially considered something of a risk. Cantona came to Old Trafford on the back of a career in France that encompassed half a dozen acrimonious partings. His liaison with Leeds had made him a crowd favourite but a manager's headache. His whole attitude screamed, "It's me against the world", and that, ironically, was an attraction for Ferguson. "It

TIMELINE

August 1992 United begin the inaugural Premier League season with a disappointing 2–1 defeat away to Sheffield United.

November 1992 On 27 November 1992, Eric Cantona joins Manchester United from Leeds United for £1.2 million.

December 1992 Cantona makes his United debut as a second-half substitute in a 2–1 derby win over Manchester City.

MANCHESTER UNITED **OFFICIAL MEMBERS' HISTORY BOOK** 117

The start of a beautiful relationship: Alex Ferguson and his new signing Eric Cantona in November 1992.

was as though he was born to be a United player", said the United boss later.

Former Liverpool captain Emlyn Hughes described the transfer as "a panic buy", and few foresaw just what an impact Cantona would have on the United team. He provided the spark that ignited the longest sustained period of success in United's history.

On 6 December 1992, the new signing made his debut, coming off the bench against Manchester City as a substitute for Ryan Giggs. One defence-splitting crossfield pass later, it was clear that cries of panic buy were somewhat off the mark. Five goals in the next six games reinforced the point and helped United to climb up the table. The victories against Coventry, Tottenham, Queen's Park Rangers, Nottingham Forest and league leaders Norwich not only indicated a new consistency but also a confidence and flair that had not always been evident before the Frenchman's arrival.

Alex Ferguson was soon moved to describe Cantona as a "model pro, an absolute dream footballer". And the work Cantona put in on the training pitch inspired his team-mates. "Eric really changed the way we viewed the game," admitted Mark Hughes. "You see Eric do things and think to yourself, 'Oh, I'll try that.' You can't expect to be as good at it as Eric is, but I think he has just freed us all a little bit."

By the end of January, the newly "freed up" United were in a three-horse title race with Aston Villa, managed by former United boss Ron Atkinson, and Norwich City.

February began in the right way with a 2–1 victory against Sheffield United. Eric was on the scoresheet along with Brian McClair, and United's resilient display provoked Blades' boss Dave Bassett to admit, "It wouldn't surprise me if they won the title."

A tough point was secured at Elland Road in a goalless draw with Leeds before United returned to winning ways with a 2–1 victory over Southampton. This time, it was 19-year-old winger Ryan Giggs who was the star, scoring both goals in a virtuoso performance. The following week, Giggs conjured up another lightning strke, launching United towards a 3–0 victory over Middlesbrough.

Even better was to come, as United began March with a trip to Anfield and a sweet away victory. Both of United's wingers, Lee Sharpe and Giggs, were on form as the visitors

TIMELINE

February 1993
A Cantona-less United side exit the FA Cup at the fifth round stage, 2–1 losers to Sheffield United at Bramall Lane.

March 1993
United earn a great 2–1 win against Liverpool at Anfield with goals by McClair and Hughes.

April 1993
United beat league leaders Norwich City 3–1 at Carrow Road, then produce a remarkable comeback to beat Sheffield Wednesday 2–1 at Old Trafford.

118   MANCHESTER UNITED OFFICIAL MEMBERS' HISTORY BOOK

enjoyed a 2–1 win.

Sharpe was another to have endured "the new Best" tag in his early days at United but, after long bouts of illness and injury, the 21 year-old was carving a niche all for himself in the United first team during the 1992/93 season with a series of excellent displays.

If victory at Anfield was a result to savour, United fans were soon brought back to earth with a surprise midweek defeat against relegation-threatened Oldham. The result cost Villa boss Atkinson a few pounds. Before the game he had phoned Oldham manager Joe Royle and claimed Oldham "didn't have the bottle" to beat local rivals United. Royle responded that Atkinson should send him a bottle of champagne if his team proved otherwise. In typically flamboyant mode, the Villa manager promised to send an entire case.

It set the scene nicely for the following weekend, when United played host to Villa at Old Trafford in a top-of-the-table clash. However, despite long periods of domination and a Mark Hughes goal, United had to settle for a point as Villa hung on for a 1–1 draw. It left both teams on 61 points, with only goal difference keeping Ferguson's side top.

Two more draws in quick succession, against Manchester City and Arsenal, meant United slipped to third before a trip to Carrow Road to face league leaders Norwich. Despite the absence of Mark Hughes through suspension, Ferguson decided to make the trip with an attacking line-up that included Giggs, Sharpe, McClair, Kanchelskis and Cantona. It proved to be the right decision as goals in the first 20 minutes from Giggs, Kanchelskis and Cantona secured victory in an enthralling match and put United back on top of the table.

United's destiny was now in their own hands. As Steve Bruce put it, "We've seven matches left and if we win them all, no-one can stop us." Bruce played a pivotal role in United's

Andrei Kanchelskis

next game, at home to Sheffield Wednesday.

With the team closing in on a first title for 26 years, tensions were running high. The Old Trafford crowd were probably more nervous than the players and Ferguson addressed the issue in his programme notes: "I have a two-word message for the players and supporters … enjoy it. We are in a marvellous position and it would be a pity if we all got so full of anxiety and worry that we failed to appreciate what we are watching."

Fine words, but they went out of the window in the 64th minute when Wednesday were awarded a penalty following Paul Ince's challenge on Chris Waddle. The spot-kick was converted by John Sheridan and Wednesday maintained their lead until four minutes from time. By that stage, fingernails had been chewed to the bone as United toiled to get something from the game.

Finally, the break came. Bruce connected with Denis Irwin's corner to bring United level, but there was more drama to come. An injury to the referee had caused a delay during the game and there was some seven minutes of added time to be played. United spent all of it seeking a winner to ensure no points were dropped in this crucial stage of the season. Six minutes and 12 seconds into injury time Old Trafford erupted as Bruce came good again, heading into the top corner from Gary Pallister's chip. Ferguson, supposedly suffering from flu was on the pitch, punching the air. Brian Kidd fell to his knees in pure relief.

Victories over Coventry, Chelsea and Crystal Palace kept United in the driving seat. Ron Atkinson's team had to beat Oldham to prevent United from being crowned champions the following day against Blackburn at Old Trafford. The game was being televised live on Sky and the United squad could only sit and wait, hoping for the right result.

May 1993
Oldham beat title contenders Aston Villa on 2 May and United are crowned league champions for the first time in 26 years!

July 1993
Roy Keane is signed from Nottingham Forest for a British record transfer fee of £3.75 million.

October 1993
United are knocked out of the European Cup by Turkish side Galatasaray. The tie finishes 3–3 on aggregate, but United lose on away goals after a stormy 0–0 draw in Istanbul.

Ferguson decided he couldn't put himself through the mill of watching the match, instead playing golf with his eldest son Mark at Mottram Hall near his home in Cheshire.

Peter Schmeichel also managed to avoid the tension for most of the 90 minutes:

"We trained on the Sunday and while Villa played Oldham, I was having a nap! When I woke up an hour later, I tuned into Teletext to see the result. Oldham were winning 1–0 but there were still five minutes to go. Those were five long minutes! And then the final whistle blew. Oldham had won! After 26 years, Manchester United were league champions again, and I was a member of the team that had done it!"

The news soon filtered on to the golf course.

"I heard a car screeching to a halt and footsteps coming up the gravel path by the green," said Ferguson. "A chap appeared with a huge smile on his face. 'Mr Ferguson?' he called, and when I turned to him he shouted, 'Manchester United have won the league.' Mark and I hugged each other, joined by the bearer of this great news. God, what a feeling!"

Meanwhile, the first and possibly only example of a pre-match party under Ferguson's reign was in full swing at Steve Bruce's house. An elated Lee Sharpe initially made his way to Old Trafford where he was mobbed by celebrating fans, but he eventually arrived at Bruce's house to join the rest of his team-mates. Serious partying was still going on the next day when the players arrived for the Blackburn Rovers match.

"There was a fantastic atmosphere when we got to the ground," said Peter Schmeichel. "Some of us were still bleary-eyed. But among all the jubilation, the manager brought us back down to earth, saying, 'We are the champions now, go out and prove it!'"

After a shaky start, they did, running out 3–1 winners in what was something of a carnival atmosphere at Old Trafford on one of the greatest days in United's history.

"It was a long time coming," recalls Bryan Robson. "But from then on, no one could throw the 26-year gap in the faces of the players. It provided the platform for the club to go forward and dominate English football."

In the following season, the team were, if anything, even hungrier for success. The entire squad redoubled its efforts, buoyed by the signing of ultra-competitive midfielder Roy Keane from Nottingham Forest for a Britsh record fee of £3.75 million. The Irish international who would come to be known simply as "Massive" by United fans made an immediate impact, scoring two goals on his home debut in a 3–0 win over Sheffield United in the second league match of the season.

Four wins and a draw in their first five games showed United were stronger than ever and for a large part of the season, they looked like running away with the league title. Meanwhile Cantona's influence continued to grow. There were 24 goals from the Frenchman during the campaign and some of them were truly sublime. For instance, in September, he ruined David Seaman's birthday visit to Old Trafford with a 25-yard rocket shot to secure a 1–0 win over Arsenal. Then there was the goal against Wimbledon in the FA Cup in February when he controlled a clearance on the edge of the area with one touch before imperiously volleying it into the net.

He also inspired a 3–2 comeback win against bitter rivals Manchester City at Maine Road; with United 2–0 down at half-time, Eric's two goals and an 87th minute winner by Roy Keane completed a sensational reversal.

Fans took to heart his comparisons of football and poetry, and his status took on mythic proportions.

"I love this club," said Cantona. "I feel really at

Roy Keane

January 1994
On 20 January, the great Sir Matt Busby dies, aged 84. Fans flock to Old Trafford to leave floral tributes, scarves and flags in his honour.

March 1994
Eric Cantona is sent off in consecutive league matches against Swindon and Arsenal. He receives a five-match ban…

March 1994
… Cantona plays in the League Cup final against Aston Villa, but to no avail as United tumble to a 3–1 defeat, ending hopes of a domestic Treble.

What a feeling: Bruce and Robson celebrate United's 1993/94 Premiership triumph.

home here. I cannot stress enough how important United fans are to me. They are really special. They make me happy, and when I'm happy, I perform."

The only blot on the landscape was elimination from the European Cup in the second round by Galatasaray. United had carelessly given away a 2–0 lead in the home leg, finishing with a 3–3 draw. A stormy but goalless second-leg match in Turkey sent the Reds spiralling out of the competition on the away goals rule.

United's stars took out their disappointment on domestic opposition. Their league form remained solid and they powered their way to the Coca-Cola Cup final with wins over Stoke City, Leicester City, Everton, Portsmouth and Sheffield Wednesday. But just before the final against Aston Villa, things started to go wrong. Cantona was sent off in consecutive league games against Swindon Town and Arsenal, matches that both ended in unconvincing 2–2 draws, and was punished with a five-match ban. Cantona wasn't suspended for the final, but he was virtually anonymous as Villa pulled off a shock 3–1 win.

Ferguson was quick to defend his French talisman over the sendings-off that were causing a media feeding frenzy:

"He knows that he was at fault for what happened at Swindon, but it's just a spark that he's got which can lead to situations like that."

"It was inevitable that Eric was going to get slated by the press, but I didn't expect to read some of the things that were written."

"He's a nutter," bellowed The Sun, proving Ferguson's point, insisting that United's subsequent loss of form would ensure that the French striker left for pastures new.

It was true that, with Cantona out of the side, results slipped and Blackburn began to put real pressure on United's title challenge. A week after the Villa defeat, sans Cantona, United lost 2–0 to Blackburn Rovers at Ewood Park with both goals scored by Alan Shearer.

Then a woeful performance against Oldham Athletic in the FA Cup semi-final nearly destroyed the Double dream. Sheffield United, Norwich and Wimbledon had all been despatched away from home before an Old Trafford victory against Charlton took United into the semi-finals, but Oldham took a 1–0 lead in extra-time. With just 46 seconds of the 120 minutes remaining, Mark Hughes volleyed a brilliant equalizer.

That "stroke of genius", as Oldham manager

May 1994
United clinch the club's first-ever league championship and FA Cup Double, by beating Chelsea 4–0 at Wembley. Cantona scores two penalties.

August 1994
United begin their defence of the league title with a solid 2–0 win over Queen's Park Rangers at Old Trafford.

September 1994
There is media uproar as Ferguson fields a young side against Port Vale in the League Cup. United win the tie 4–1 on aggregate, with unknown Paul Scholes scoring two.

Joe Royle called it, proved to be the turning point. "Forcing a replay gave us a second chance of reaching the final," said Hughes. "We were not going to let that opportunity slip."

United destroyed Oldham 4–1, Cantona returned from suspension and United's league form picked up again. A 2–1 win over Ipswich on 1 May and Coventry's 2–1 win over Blackburn a day later confirmed United as champions again.

But to win the Double, they would have to beat Chelsea in the FA Cup final, the only team to beat the Reds home and away in the league that year. On a rainy day at Wembley, United won 4–0. A stunning second-half display that included two penalties by Cantona, a Mark Hughes goal and a 90th minute tap-in by Brian McClair topped off an historic season.

Sadly, one legend did not witness the triumphant climax to the Double season. On 20 January 1994, Sir Matt Busby died, aged 84. Fans flocked to Old Trafford to pay tribute to the man who had done so much for the club and the ground was awash with floral tributes and scarves and flags.

Alex Ferguson summed up the thoughts of many, saying: "I found him a wonderful and incredible man, a character of substance and charisma. There have been some outstanding managers in this country, but without doubt he is the greatest ever."

With the memory of the historic double still fresh in the minds of fans, the 1994/95 campaign began with a keen sense of anticipation. It proved to be a dramatic season, but not in a way anyone foresaw.

Kung-fu Eric

On 25 January 1995, United went to London to play Crystal Palace. It should have been a routine fixture. Palace were fighting what turned out to be a lost cause, avoiding relegation; United were trying to make up ground on Blackburn in the title race.

For the first 45 minutes, the game was indeed a typically wintry, blood and guts Premiership encounter – no goals, few chances but plenty of crunching challenges. In particular, Palace's central defenders Richard Shaw and Chris Coleman were struggling to control United's new signing Andrew Cole and Cantona and their efforts to deal with the striking duo were causing Ferguson some consternation.

"Some of the tackles were disgraceful," he said. "The referee Alan Wilkie's inability to stamp them out made subsequent trouble unavoidable. I spoke to him about it before the second half, but he looked at me as if I had horns on my head."

During the interval, Ferguson warned Eric Cantona not to be tempted into any retaliation, but the advice fell on deaf ears. Not for the first time, an aggrieved Eric decided to take the law into his own hands. Four minutes into the second half, he blatantly kicked Shaw, and referee Wilkie decided this was as good a time as any to become an authoritarian. Eric was given his marching orders for the fifth time in a United shirt and the headline writers had their back-page lead. A minute later, the story had moved to the front page.

Cantona was being escorted off the pitch by United kitman Norman Davies. "At first, we were walking along the pitch," he recalls, "but a steward insisted we move over to the touchline. At Selhurst Park, that puts you close to the fans. The abuse Eric was getting was pretty nasty."

Matthew Simmons ran down 11 rows of seats to get to the front. "It's an early shower for you, Cantona," was his recollection of what he said. Even allowing for a blip in translation, the outburst still seems somewhat removed from what Eric claimed to have heard, which was a racist tirade aimed at him and his mother.

Cantona snapped. He lunged two-footed into the crowd and proceeded to swap punches with a shaken Simmons who had never imagined there might be some payback

TIMELINE

December 1994
David Beckham scores his first senior goal in a 4–0 thrashing of Galatasaray, but the win is insufficient to prevent United's elimination from the newly formed Champions League.

January 1995
Andy Cole signs for United for £6 million plus Keith Gillespie who goes to Newcastle United in part exchange.

January 1995
On 25 January 1995, Eric Cantona tries to literally kick racism out of football, kung-fu kicking a fan who abuses him after being sent-off at Crystal Palace.

The victorious 1993/94 Double-winning team show off their trophies during a celebratory bus parade in Manchester.

for his outburst. The police moved in, Paul Ince allegedly offered to take on the entire crowd and Peter Schmeichel dragged Eric away.

The second half re-commenced, a 1–1 draw the final result, but behind the scenes, events were still unfolding.

"When Eric got to the dressing-room, he said nothing but you could sense he knew how serious it was," said Ferguson. "All the other players came in after the game and went into the showers and still he sat there in the corner of the room. We were called into the referee's room to talk to the police. The inspector said, 'There are a lot of allegations flying around and we must investigate them thoroughly. But we are not going to get hysterical about this.'"

The media had no such concerns. *The Sun's* 13-page report on 'The Shame of Cantona' was just the start. Revelation followed revelation over the next few weeks, and for a while it looked as though Eric would go either into exile or to jail – or worse join Inter Milan.

When the dust settled, Eric was left with an eight-month ban from football and a jail sentence, subsequently commuted to 120 hours' community service. Without him, United ended the season trophyless, losing the FA Cup final by a single goal to Everton and the league by a point to Blackburn Rovers. Striker Andrew Cole, who had joined for a British record £6 million fee from Newcastle was unfairly made the critics' scapegoat for United's narrow failure to retain the league title, even though he'd scored 12 goals in 17 games since his January transfer (including a record-breaking five in one game against Ipswich Town).

During the summer, there was further drama after the FA tried to stop Cantona from joining in training matches. The Frenchman decided enough was enough and went back to France. Fortunately, Alex Ferguson flew to Paris to persuade his player to stay on at United. After a few hours of talks, Eric agreed to do so.

The suspension still had a few months to run and Ferguson began the season with a number of his younger squad members pushed to the fore. Controversially, he had sold Mark Hughes, Paul Ince and Andrei Kanchelskis during the close season. Many fans questioned Ferguson's wisdom in selling three big-name stars, but he had faith in the home-grown talent nurtured within United's youth system. The departures

March 1995
Cantona is sentenced to two weeks' imprisonment. The sentence is later commuted to 120 hours of community service.

May 1995
Without Cantona, United lose the league title to Blackburn Rovers by a point. United are also beaten 1–0 by Everton in the FA Cup final.

August 1995
Having controversially sold Hughes, Ince and Kanchelskis in summer, Ferguson fields a young side to play Aston Villa on the opening day of the season. United lose 3–1.

King Eric caps a double Double-winning 1995/96 season by lifting the FA Cup at Wembley.

created opportunities for the likes of David Beckham, Nicky Butt and Paul Scholes.

Defeat in the opening game of the season at Aston Villa did little to show the promise of "Fergie's Fledglings". Television commentator Alan Hansen went so far as to claim, "You'll never win anything with kids."

However, consecutive league wins against West Ham, Wimbledon, Blackburn, Everton and Bolton quickly proved that the manager's faith in his youth system was justified as United moved to their now familiar place at the top of the table.

Sadly, European glory still seemed out of reach with an early exit from the UEFA Cup at the hands of Rotor Volgograd (despite Peter Schmeichel scoring a goal!). There was also a shock 4–3 aggregate defeat by York City in the League Cup. But before too much gloom could set in, Eric returned.

On 1 October 1995, after an absence of 248 days, United's French star was back at Old Trafford. He received a frenzied reception on his return and the celebrations were to continue for the rest of the season, as a new, improved Eric Cantona cemented his reputation as one of the truly great players. In his first game back, against Liverpool, and

wearing his trademark No.7 shirt, it took the Gallic genius just 67 seconds to set up a goal for Nicky Butt and later he scored himself to salvage a 2–2 draw.

As the title race picked up speed, it was the Frenchman who ensured United finished ahead of the pack. Surrounded by a number of young players with more talent than experience, Eric, now wearing the captain's armband, was to prove a rock of consistency. Some 13 games that season were decided by a Cantona winner or equalizer as he practically dragged the team to a third Premiership title and a Wembley date with Liverpool in the FA Cup final. In their last 23 Premiership and FA Cup games, United lost just once, scoring 46 goals and conceding 13. The Reds finished off their league campaign in style, demolishing Nottingham Forest 5–0 at home in the penultimate game of the season and clinching the title with a 3–0 win at Middlesbrough.

Cantona was voted Footballer of the Year by the very journalists who had demanded his departure only a year earlier.

But the defining moment of Eric's rehabilitation came at Wembley Stadium in the 85th minute of the Cup final. As though in slow motion, he contorted his body to hit the

TIMELINE

September 1995
More European disappointment as United go out of the UEFA Cup on away goals to Rotor Volgograd.

October 1995
The King returns: on the first day of the month, after an absence of 248 days, Eric plays against Liverpool, providing a goal assist and a goal in a 2–2 draw.

May 1996
United win the league again, Cantona is voted the Football Writers' Footballer of the Year and he scores the FA Cup-winning goal to beat Liverpool and clinch an historic double Double.

winning goal through a sea of Liverpool players. Cantona's rehabilitation was complete. "You'll never win the Double with kids," sang joyous Reds with heavy irony to herald the team's astonishing achievement – Manchester United had become the first team ever to do the Double twice.

There was to be one final season in a red shirt for Cantona. It began in spectacular fashion for United, courtesy of David Beckham. The youngster who eventually inherited Eric's No.7 shirt, decided to win the goal of the season on the very first matchday. United had travelled to London to begin their campaign with a game against Wimbledon. It ended with a comfortable 3–0 win, but the talking point was Beckham's goal, a stunning 57-yard shot from the halfway line. Overnight, Beckham became a household name.

There were several new faces at Old Trafford. Ferguson had been busy in the transfer market and there were five arrivals – Karel Poborsky, Jordi Cruyff, Ole Gunnar Solskjaer, Ronny Johnsen and Raimond Van Der Gouw.

In the European Cup, United were defeated twice by Juventus, but did enough against Rapid Vienna and Fenerbahçe to ensure qualification for the quarter-finals where they were due to meet Porto.

The home tie decided it; in a 4–0 demolition of the visitors, United truly fulfilled their potential. It was a breathtaking display of counter-attacking football. David May, Ryan Giggs, Andy Cole and Cantona were the scorers on one of those glorious European nights at Old Trafford.

Meanwhile, in the league, despite squad rotation to keep players fresh for Europe, United were again dominating. Wins over Coventry, Sheffield Wednesday and Everton ensured that they finished March six points clear at the top of the table.

In April, they consolidated their league position, but there was disappointment in

Europe. Despite outplaying Borussia Dortmund home and away, poor finishing robbed United, 0–2 aggregate losers, of a chance to appear in the European Cup final. It was a bitter pill to swallow, and even the following month's triumph in the league provided little consolation. United were champions again, but still craved the ultimate prize – the European Cup.

It was the end of the road for Cantona, who shocked football by deciding he'd had enough. At 30 years-old, he quit the game for good at the end of the season, deciding his magnificent powers had peaked. "I don't want to be a player who leaves a big club to play in the lower divisions," he once said. "Manchester United will be my last club."

Nonetheless, his departure came as a shock, even to his team-mates.

"Jordi Cruyff and I went to London for the weekend with our girlfriends," said Ole Gunnar Solskjaer. "And as we boarded the train back from Euston a British Rail officer told us the news. I didn't believe it at first, neither did Jordi.

"In 30 or 40 years' time, I'll boast about having played with Eric. Even before I came to the club, I looked up to him and admired his skills. And I admire him even more now, after I've trained with him and got to know him as a person. He was a huge influence at the club and gave everyone a lift with his presence. That is what I'll miss most of all."

Cantona had provided the catalyst to end United's 26-year championship drought and had helped build the foundations of a team that would go on to challenge – and beat – Europe's finest. As a former 'King' of Old Trafford, Denis Law, observed, "Eric was the missing piece of the jigsaw that Alex was searching for."

Eric was gone, but his legacy lived on, as United would demonstrate two seasons later in the most dramatic fashion imaginable.

David Beckham

August 1996
United start the season with five new players in the squad including Ole Gunnar Solskjaer. David Beckham scores an incredible 57-yard goal against Wimbledon in the first league game.

April 1997
United disappointingly lose 2–0 on aggregate in the Champions League semi-final against Borussia Dortmund.

May 1997
United win the league title for the fourth time under Alex Ferguson, but the triumph is soon overshadowed by Eric Cantona's decision to retire from football at the age of 30.

MANCHESTER UNITED **OFFICIAL MEMBERS' HISTORY BOOK**   125

On 26 May 1999, Alex Ferguson and his Treble-winning heroes reached the promised land.

CHAPTER FOURTEEN

NAME ON THE TROPHY...

Eric Cantona's retirement left fans wondering how the team would cope without the King. But the Red juggernaut powered on, and just two years later the new United would rewrite football history...

How on earth would United replace Eric Cantona? That was the question every United supporter was asking in the summer of 1997. The charismatic Frenchman's retirement left a gaping hole not only in the team, but also in the hearts of thousands of his Red disciples.

Manager Alex Ferguson was widely expected to look abroad for a world-class successor to Cantona. But while Italian club Internazionale splashed out £16.5 million to buy Ronaldo, Ferguson invested a paltry £3.5 million in Tottenham Hotspur and England star Teddy Sheringham. At 31, Sheringham was also the same age as the retired Frenchman, and fans wondered whether he too was past his peak.

Sheringham was given his favourite No. 10 squad number while the previous incumbent, David Beckham, gratefully slipped into Cantona's No. 7 shirt. Meanwhile, Alex Ferguson handed the captain's armband to Roy Keane.

United's first league fixture was against Spurs and Teddy Sheringham received a hostile reception on his return to White Hart Lane. Sheringham's second-half penalty hit the post to the unadulterated joy of home fans, but a late Nicky Butt strike and a Ramon Vega own goal gifted United a 2–0 win.

A day later, United announced the £5 million signing of central defender Henning Berg from Blackburn Rovers.

Following the hard-fought win at Spurs, United played solid but uninspiring football in the league for the first two months of the season. The most significant incident of this period occurred during a 0–1 defeat by Leeds at Elland Road when captain Roy Keane injured cruciate knee ligaments making a rash challenge on Leeds midfielder Alf-Inge Haaland. That one moment of frustration put Keane out of action for the rest of the season.

No Cantona and now no Keane – could United cope without two such influential figures? The early signs were positive. In late October, Andy Cole fired in a hat-trick in the 7–0 demolition of Barnsley and Sheffield Wednesday were blown away by goals from Cole, Sheringham (two) and Ole Gunnar Solskjaer (two) in a 6–1 drubbing.

By the turn of the year, United were top of the Premiership with 46 points from 21 games, five points clear of Blackburn Rovers with Arsenal languishing a distant 12 points behind in sixth place. United's dominant form was confirmed on 4 January when they travelled to Stamford Bridge to play Chelsea in the FA Cup third round. On paper, it looked a tough tie against a team then lying third in the Premiership, but Chelsea were simply overpowered as goals from Beckham (two), Cole (two) and Sheringham put United 5–0 up after 75 minutes. The Blues scored three late goals, but afterwards manager Gianluca Vialli conceded that they had been out-classed.

"This United team is one of the finest Europe has seen," he said.

Ferguson's men had still to prove it by winning the European Cup though. The team's form in the group phases of the Champions

TIMELINE

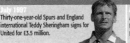

July 1997
Thirty-one-year-old Spurs and England international Teddy Sheringham signs for United for £3.5 million.

August 1997
After having previous bids turned down, Alex Ferguson finally gets his man, buying Blackburn Rovers and Norway defender Henning Berg for £5 million.

September 1997
United's new captain Roy Keane injures cruciate ligaments making a rash challenge on Leeds midfielder Alf-Inge Haaland and is ruled out for the season.

Genius at work: Ryan Giggs on his way to scoring an extraordinary individual goal to clinch a 2–1 extra-time win over Arsenal in the 1999 FA Cup semi-final replay.

League had been encouraging with five wins in six matches and there was a Champions League quarter-final against AS Monaco to look forward to in March. Before then, United had Premiership and FA Cup affairs to attend to in January and February. But rather than build on that sensational Chelsea win, there were surprise single-goal defeats by Southampton away and Leicester City at home. Dreams of a Treble were shattered by lowly Barnsley who knocked out a below-strength United side 3–2 in the FA Cup fifth-round replay. Even a 2–0 league victory against Derby County at Old Trafford had a sting in the tail as Ryan Giggs limped off with a hamstring injury that would rule him out of the Monaco tie.

The first leg against Monaco (who had a certain Fabien Barthez in goal) was played on an appalling pitch at the Stade Louis II that stopped either team from playing flowing football and ended in a 0–0 stalemate.

Four days before the return match, United faced a vital league game at home to Arsenal. The resurgent Gunners produced a powerful performance to beat a jaded United side 1–0. Worse still, goalkeeper Peter Schmeichel tore his hamstring after a mad dash upfield for a corner in the final minute.

Alex Ferguson's injury list had reached critical levels. He fielded an XI against Monaco at Old Trafford minus Schmeichel, Giggs, Keane and Gary Pallister. Ultimately, Monaco striker David Trezeguet's 96mph rocket shot after just five minutes proved vital. Ole Gunnar Solskjaer made it 1–1 on 53 minutes, but Monaco held out to win on away goals.

"I've never felt so low in football," said Alex Ferguson. "If we'd had a full side I'm sure we would have gone on, but in retrospect I should have tried harder to find cover for Ryan Giggs."

Now there was just the Premiership to play for, but by the end of March, Arsenal were six points behind the Reds with three games in hand. United continued to battle bravely, but their usual slick passing game had given way to hopeful punts forward – consecutive 1–1 draws at home to Liverpool and Newcastle in April highlighted United's deficiencies.

TIMELINE

January 1998
United trounce Chelsea 5–3 in the FA Cup third round, the Reds best performance of the season.

March 1998
United crash out of the Champions League on away goals after a 1–1 aggregate draw with AS Monaco.

May 1998
Arsenal complete an 11-game winning streak to clinch the Premiership title, with two United fixtures still remaining.

On 2 May, Arsenal completed an amazing 11-game winning streak with a 4–0 thrashing of Everton at Highbury to claim the Premiership title and render United's two remaining fixtures irrelevant. The Gunners went on to claim their second double, beating Newcastle 2–0 in the FA Cup final at Wembley.

Although United's failure to win anything in 1997/98 was mainly caused by injuries to key players, Alex Ferguson knew he had to strengthen his squad. Indeed, he'd secured an agreement from PSV Eindhoven to sell Jaap Stam to United before that campaign had even finished. The massive Dutch international central defender officially signed on 1 July for £10.75 million, a world record transfer fee for a defender. Ferguson also fulfilled his promise to buy high-quality cover for Ryan Giggs by signing 24-year-old Swedish international Jesper Blomqvist from Parma for £4.5 million.

It was also time to say goodbye to some members of the old guard with Gary Pallister and Brian McClair leaving Manchester United after a combined 20 years of service.

United's pre-season preparations culminated with a chance to gain revenge over league champions Arsenal in the Charity Shield match. Instead, the Reds were soundly thrashed 3–0. The only consolation for United supporters was the sight of captain Roy Keane playing again after a 10-month lay-off.

United bounced back with an easy 2–0 aggregate win over LKS Lodz in the Champions League preliminary round that saw the team through to the group phase.

They began their league campaign with a 2–2 draw against Leicester City at Old Trafford. Before the next fixture away to West Ham, United finally completed the £12.6 million signing of Aston Villa striker Dwight Yorke, thus ending months of feverish media speculation.

Yorke made little impression against West Ham and the game ended goalless, but he scored two in the 4–1 drubbing of newly promoted Charlton Athletic four days later. However, Yorke's performance that night was largely over-shadowed by the news that BSkyB's £623 million takeover bid for United had been accepted by the club board. Many fans were against the move and following a Monopolies and Mergers Commission investigation, the Department of Trade and Industry eventually blocked the deal.

United's season warmed up in September with consecutive matches against Barcelona, Arsenal, Liverpool and Bayern Munich. The 3–3 draw against Barcelona at Old Trafford was the first classic of the season. Giggs and Scholes gave United a 2–0 half-time lead. After the interval, Barca launched a fierce comeback and made it 2–2. A beautiful Beckham free-kick on 64 minutes restored United's advantage, but the visitors earned a deserved draw with a Luis Enrique penalty after Nicky Butt had handled the ball in a goalmouth scramble.

Nicky Butt was sent off for that offence and four days later he was shown another red card as United subsided to an inglorious 0–3 away defeat by Arsenal. There was no respite for the Reds who took on Liverpool next at Old Trafford – this time they eased to a 2–0 win.

In the final game of this tough four-game stretch, a last-minute mistake by goalkeeper Peter Schmeichel in the Olympic Stadium let in Bayern Munich striker Elber to grab a 2–2 draw, but United bounced back to thrash Schmeichel's former club Brondby IF 6–2 (away) and 5–0 (home) in their next two Champions League outings.

The team's momentum was starting to build in the Premiership too, and by the end of October, United were second in the table. The only worry was the indifferent form of Peter Schmeichel, but the Great Dane's announcement on 12 November 1998 that he

Dwight Yorke

July 1998
Giant PSV Eindhoven and Dutch international defender Jaap Stam signs for £10.75 million, a world record fee for a defender.

August 1998
After months of media speculation, United finally sign Dwight Yorke from Aston Villa for £12.6 million.

September 1998
United fans enjoy the first classic match of the season, a 3–3 draw against Barcelona at Old Trafford in the Champions League.

MANCHESTER UNITED **OFFICIAL MEMBERS' HISTORY BOOK**   129

"Who put the ball in the Germans' net? O-le Gun-nar Solsk-jaer!"

intended to quit Manchester United at the end of the season still came as a massive shock.

Another thrilling 3–3 draw against Barcelona, this time at the Nou Camp, was the highlight of November, but the team's form slumped dramatically during the Christmas period. In December, the Reds record read: one win, five draws and two defeats. The prime reason for this poor run can be traced to the departure of assistant manager Brian Kidd on 4 December. After years of sterling service to the club both as a player and coach, 'Kiddo' decided to try his hand at management with Blackburn Rovers.

But five wins out of five in January showed the team was back on track. Most memorable of these victories was the 2–1 home win over Liverpool in the FA Cup fourth round. They were 1–0 down to a third-minute goal by Michael Owen and looked destined for defeat with just a few minutes remaining. But an 88th-minute tap-in by Dwight Yorke and a last-gasp winner by substitute Ole Gunnar Solskjaer clinched a remarkable victory.

In February, Alex Ferguson brought in Steve McClaren from Derby County as his new assistant manager. McClaren's new club battered relegation-bound Nottingham Forest 8–1 at the City Ground in his first game. That day, after watching Andrew Cole and Dwight Yorke score two goals apiece, Ole Gunnar Solskjaer came on as a late substitute and scored four goals in 11 minutes (80, 88, 90, 90).

By the beginning of March, United were four points clear of Chelsea in the Premiership and attention turned to the Champions League quarter-final match against Milan giants Internazionale. Inter's Brazilian superstar Ronaldo missed the first leg in Manchester through injury and the stage was clear for Dwight Yorke to give a world-class striking display. Twice in the first half, Yorke capitalized on pinpoint crosses from David Beckham to head in the goals that clinched a 2–0 win. It was a particularly sweet night for Beckham who was up against Diego Simeone for the first time since the Argentinian's

theatrics cost him a red card in the World Cup the previous summer.

Ronaldo was deemed fit to start the return leg at the San Siro, but United showed the skill and fighting qualities of true champions. Ronaldo was expertly policed by Henning Berg and substituted after an hour. Nicola Ventola finally broke through for Inter in the 63rd minute and only a mixture of luck and Schmeichel's brilliance stopped Inter grabbing an aggregate equalizer before the tension was dissipated by Paul Scholes' late goal.

United faced old rivals Juventus in the semi-finals. Trailing 1–0 in the home leg to an Antonio Conte goal, United were struggling, but yet again their never-say-die spirit saved them. With the final whistle imminent, substitute Teddy Sheringham's flick-on set up Ryan Giggs to fire home the equalizer.

United's next game was an FA Cup semi-

TIMELINE

October 1998
United crank up the goal power scoring 19 goals in five matches, including a 6–2 thrashing of Brondby in the Champions League.

November 1998
On 12 November, Peter Schmeichel announces his intention to quit Manchester United at the end of the season citing the physical demands of the Premiership as the main factor behind his decision.

December 1998
On 4 December, 1968 European Cup-winner Brian Kidd leaves his job as assistant manager to become manager of Blackburn Rovers.

132   MANCHESTER UNITED OFFICIAL MEMBERS' HISTORY BOOK

What a feeling: the United squad celebrate winning an unprecedented Treble at the Nou Camp in May 1999.

final against Arsenal which ended 0–0. The replay three days later was an all-time classic.

A superb curling shot from David Beckham gave United the lead in the 17th minute. Arsenal struck back through Dennis Bergkamp's deflected shot on 69 minutes and then disaster struck as Roy Keane was sent off by referee David Elleray. Down to 10 men and with seconds of normal time remaining, Phil Neville felled Ray Parlour and Elleray pointed to the penalty spot. Arsenal were one kick away from the FA Cup final. Bergkamp stepped up and hit it well only for Schmeichel to save brilliantly. Extra-time arrived and with it the highlight of an astonishing match.

"It was always going to take something special to separate these two teams," said Ferguson afterwards. And how! Pouncing on a poor pass by Patrick Vieira in the 109th minute, Ryan Giggs proceeded to dance 70 yards past five defenders before unleashing a ferocious drive into the top of the net. Pandemonium followed; neither the fans nor players could believe what they'd just witnessed. Arsenal were broken and United were in the Cup final.

A week later, United produced another miracle in the Champions League semi-final second leg against Juventus.

Juve had the valuable advantage of an away goal from the first match, and a difficult proposition for United looked impossible after two goals in the first 12 minutes scored by Filippo Inzaghi put the Italians 3–1 ahead on aggregate.

United had never won on Italian soil before this night, but if the players were concerned, they didn't let it show. Skipper Roy Keane led the comeback with a captain's performance that later prompted Ferguson to say, "It's an

January 1999
Last-gasp goals by Yorke and Solskjaer turn a 1–0 deficit into a 2–1 win over Liverpool in the FA Cup fourth round.

February 1999
Alex Ferguson appoints Steve McClaren as his new number two. Ferguson had been impressed by the forward-thinking coach's work at Derby County.

February 1999
Substitute Ole Gunnar Solskjaer scores four goals in 11 minutes in an 8–1 win away to Nottingham Forest. It's the most goals ever scored by a sub and the quickest four goals ever scored by one player.

MANCHESTER UNITED **OFFICIAL MEMBERS' HISTORY BOOK**   **133**

honour to be associated with such a player."

Keane's 24th minute header pulled United back into the match. Here was a team who simply didn't believe they could be beaten. Dwight Yorke confirmed the point 10 minutes later with an adroit header from Andrew Cole's cross. It was 2–2 on the night and United were now ahead on away goals.

The Italians tried to fight back and came close on several occasions, but Jaap Stam and Peter Schmeichel stood tall to deny them. Six minutes from time, Cole made sure of matters, sliding the ball home from a tight angle after Yorke had been felled. The only sadness on a great night was that bookings for both Roy Keane and Paul Scholes ruled them out of the final against Bayern Munich.

With two cup finals to look forward to, United had to concentrate on regaining the league title. The run-in included a visit to Anfield, where Liverpool fans waved Bayern flags and celebrated as if they had won the league when Paul Ince scored an 89th-minute goal to snatch a 2–2 draw. A goalless draw in the penultimate fixture at Ewood Park consigned Brian Kidd's Blackburn Rovers team to relegation.

With Arsenal pushing the Reds all the way to the finishing line, United's 78 goals in 37 games to date would count for little if they didn't get a result against Tottenham at Old Trafford in the final Premiership fixture.

Sir Alex Ferguson

The home side were caught out by a Les Ferdinand goal in the 25th minute, so once again, United would have to come back from behind. David Beckham soothed the fans' nerves just before half-time with an angled drive past Ian Walker. One United goal in the second 45 minutes would secure United's fifth title under Alex Ferguson. It was Andy Cole who provided it. Having come on as substitute, he neatly controlled Gary Neville's pass before beautifully dinking it over Walker. United were champions again, and just two matches away from rewriting football history.

United were unstoppable and Newcastle were effortlessly dismissed 2–0 in the FA Cup final. Teddy Sheringham came on as a ninth-minute substitute for injured captain Roy Keane and 96 seconds later he was on the scoresheet, after an expert one-two with Ole Gunnar Solskjaer and a cool finish past Newcastle keeper Steve Harper.

Man of the match Sheringham also provided the assist for United's second goal on 52 minutes, laying the ball off to Paul Scholes who netted with a low drive from the edge of the penalty box.

In the dressing room afterwards, the team took great delight in singing, "Oh Teddy, Teddy, came to Man United and he won the lot!" But for that to be strictly true, there was another victory required.

On 26 May 1999, 45,000 Reds packed into the Nou Camp to see if United could win the European Cup for the first time since 1968. That day the club took out a full-page advert in a national newspaper. It was one-word long and said simply: 'Believe'.

Of course, after the dramatic triumphs of the last few matches, belief in the United team was at an all-time high. But with both Keane and Scholes suspended, Ferguson was forced to shuffle his pack. David Beckham moved into central midfield to partner Nicky Butt, while Ryan Giggs moved onto the right wing and Jesper Blomqvist played on the left.

The formation didn't seem to suit United with the Germans having the better of the first half and taking the lead after just six minutes from a Mario Basler free-kick. Ferguson's side improved in the second-half but still lacked penetration and could have fallen further behind. Schmeichel made saves to keep out

March 1999
United beat Internazionale 3–1 on aggregate in the Champions League quarter-finals.

April 1999
Ten-man United win an exhilarating FA Cup semi-final replay against Arsenal. A miraculous individual goal by Ryan Giggs snatches a 2–1 win in extra-time.

April 1999
A week after beating Arsenal, United produce another amazing comeback, beating Juventus 3–2 from 2–0 down in the Stadio Delle Alpi.

Stefan Effenberg and Mehmet Scholl. Even more alarming was Scholl's chip against the post in the 79th minute. Then, five minutes later, Carsten Jancker's overhead kick crashed against the bar.

UEFA officials had already attached Bayern Munich's colours to the trophy as the final minutes approached. Yorke and substitutes Sheringham and Solskjaer had chances but the ball wouldn't go in the net. By now United needed a miracle. It came in injury time. United won a corner and, in desperation, Schmeichel ran up to join the attack.

The big goalie's appearance confused the German markers and Beckham's corner entered a mass of bodies. Ryan Giggs mis-hit a shot that Sheringham managed to steer into the net. United fans in the stadium were delirious and television viewers back home heard ITV commentator Clive Tyldesley shout, "Name on the trophy!"

With the Germans still reeling, United won another corner. Again Beckham swung the ball in, this time Sheringham headed the ball across goal and Solskjaer poked it into the Germans' net for the second time in a matter of seconds. Bayern's players and fans were destroyed, United's ecstatic. It was a suitably impossible ending to an unbelievable season.

After the team had been presented with the trophy, the celebrations continued for 45 joyful minutes on the pitch as United fans hailed their heroes. Afterwards, the players showered, dressed and moved on to the ballroom at the Arts Hotel, partying until 5am with friends and family.

The next day they flew back with the trophy and were taken on an open-topped bus parade of Manchester. An estimated 750,000 people poured into the city centre to glimpse arguably the greatest English league team ever.

Sometime after the roar of celebration had quietened to a satisfied purr Alex Ferguson reflected that there was a sense of destiny about that famous night at the Nou Camp.

"It felt like it was meant to be. The fact that it would have been Matt Busby's 90th birthday; the fact that we were playing Munich with everything that means to this club – people who believe in God might see a pattern in that. I mean, I believe, I pray a lot. You have to sense that it all has a meaning."

May 1999
United beat Tottenham 2–1 in the final league game of the season to win the Premiership...

May 1999
... and follow up with a 2–0 victory over Newcastle in the FA Cup final to clinch the Double...

May 1999
... then 'SAS' substitutes Teddy Sheringham and Ole Gunnar Solskjaer score in added time to beat Bayern Munich in the European Cup final and complete an unprecedented Treble.

Since joining the club in 2001,
Ruud van Nistelrooy has earned
comparisons with the greatest
strikers in United's history.

CHAPTER FIFTEEN

RUUD AWAKENING

Since winning an unprecedented Treble, some of the heroes of '99 have moved on. But new players, led by Dutch ace Ruud van Nistelrooy, have joined the Reds' continuing quest to win major trophies...

After the greatest season ever, anything else was bound to be an anti-climax, but newly knighted manager Sir Alex Ferguson was determined that his team would continue their unrelenting quest for honours. "Now, we're playing for pride, our place in the history of the game," he asserted. "My players understand that."

The toughest task was to replace goalkeeper Peter Schmeichel who had left for Portuguese club Sporting Lisbon. In the summer, Mark Bosnich arrived on a free transfer from Aston Villa. But the Australian made an unfortunate start to his second spell at Old Trafford. He was injured in United's third league match, a 2–0 win over Leeds United, and Raimond Van der Gouw took his place.

By the end of August 1999, Bosnich had been relegated to third-choice keeper behind new signing Massimo Taibi (£4.5 million from Venezia) and Van der Gouw. Taibi made a promising debut behind another new signing, Mikael Silvestre, in the 3–2 triumph at Liverpool. But Taibi's howlers in a 3–3 home draw against Southampton and in the 5–0 humiliation at Chelsea allowed Bosnich to regain his place by early October.

A month later, Bosnich's brilliance was the key to Manchester United's 1–0 victory over Palmeiras in the annual Intercontinental Cup match between the champions of Europe and South America.

"I used to watch that game in Australia and it was a big thing." recalled Bosnich. "We knew no British team had won it in its 39-year history and we really wanted to be the first."

Despite the unsettled goalkeeping situation, United were the dominant attacking force in domestic football throughout 1999/2000. Highlights included the 5–1 annihilation of Newcastle United (with Andy Cole scoring four against his old club) and the 7–1 thrashing of West Ham in April (including a Paul Scholes hat-trick). United scored a Premiership record-breaking 97 goals in 38 matches, gathering a total of 91 points to finish a massive 18 points clear of second-placed Arsenal.

Unfortunately, it was impossible for United to repeat their Treble success because the club didn't enter the FA Cup. The controversial decision to play in the inaugural FIFA Club World Championship instead was made under government pressure to support England's 2006 World Cup bid.

So while FA Cup third-round matches were being played in the English winter, United appeared in the searing heat of Rio de Janeiro. United drew their opening match with Mexican side Necaxa, then lost to Brazilian team Vasco Da Gama and were thus eliminated in the group phase.

With the disappointment of Brazil forgotten, United showed the potential to retain the European Cup in the second group-phase match against Fiorentina in mid-March, beating Gabriel Batistuta and co. 3–1 at Old Trafford.

But the Reds couldn't sustain their form in the quarter-final against Spanish giants Real Madrid. Only Bosnich's resilience allowed

TIMELINE

July 1999
Goalkeeper Mark Bosnich joins United on a free transfer from Aston Villa. Bosnich had briefly played for United in the early Nineties.

August 1999
Another goalkeeper, Massimo Taibi, is signed from Venezia for £4.5 million.

September 1999
French defender Mikael Silvestre, 22, joins United from Internazionale for £3.5 million.

MANCHESTER UNITED **OFFICIAL MEMBERS' HISTORY BOOK**   137

United to escape from the first leg with a 0–0 draw. But Bosnich wasn't fit to play in the return, and Madrid exploited United's defensive uncertainty, racing to a 3–0 lead before the hour. Despite a valiant fightback, in which Beckham and Scholes narrowed the scoreline to 2–3, United crashed out of the European Cup to the eventual winners.

The following season, United continued their domestic supremacy as Sir Alex Ferguson became the first manager ever to lead the same team to three consecutive league titles. The championship race was effectively over by January – a 3–1 win over West Ham on New Year's Day put the Reds 11 points clear and they never looked like surrendering their lead.

With redevelopment work on Old Trafford completed, capacity 67,000-plus crowds were regularly treated to scintillating displays as the likes of Teddy Sheringham, Andy Cole and Ole Gunnar Solskjaer all struck a rich vein of goalscoring form. United saved their most savage beating for fierce rivals Arsenal in February. The Gunners were thrashed 6–1, with Dwight Yorke grabbing a hat-trick.

The season will also be remembered for the emergence of a new United cult hero in the shape of World Cup-winning goalkeeper Fabien Barthez. Signed from Monaco in the summer of 2000, the eccentric Frenchman immediately displaced Mark Bosnich (Bosnich later joined Chelsea) and captured United fans' imagination with his athleticism, distribution and penchant for dribbling past opposing forwards!

Still, United could not recapture the glories of 1999. The Reds' return to FA Cup competition was short-lived as they were defeated 1–0 at Old Trafford by a plucky West Ham side. And United disappointed again in Europe. In the quarter-finals they were outfought and out-thought by a strong Bayern Munich team. Desperate for revenge after 1999, Bayern ran out 3–1 aggregate winners.

"I have seen United players getting complacent, thinking they've done it all and getting carried away by a bit of success," warned skipper Roy Keane. "All you have to do is drop your standards slightly and it's obvious, especially in Europe."

The 2001/02 season was supposed to be Sir Alex Ferguson's final fling before retirement and he was clearly determined to finish his glittering career on a high. A European Cup final victory at Hampden Park in his native Glasgow topped the agenda.

To meet the challenge, Argentina's Juan Sebastian Veron was snapped up in a £28 million deal, while Dutch striker Ruud van Nistelrooy arrived from PSV Eindhoven for £19 million and goalkeeper Roy Carroll signed from Wigan Athletic.

Van Nistelrooy shone immediately with a brace in the 3–2 home victory over Fulham on the opening day of the season. But for some time United had appeared shaky in defence and Sir Alex replaced Lazio-bound Jaap Stam with French veteran Laurent Blanc.

Throughout the campaign United upheld the traditions of attacking play, with Van Nistelrooy proving to be a world-class act.

Juan Sebastian Veron

Highlights included recovering from a three-goal deficit at White Hart Lane to beat Tottenham Hotspur 5–3 in September 2001 and the 3–0 demolition of Chelsea at Stamford Bridge the following April.

Van Nistelrooy's success precipitated the departure of Andy Cole, who signed for Blackburn Rovers in December 2001. United brought in Uruguayan striker Diego Forlan (£7 million from Independiente) as Cole's replacement a month later.

Unfortunately, the defence continued to leak goals – 45 in total in the Premiership – as United suffered nine defeats, including embarrassing reverses against Bolton and

TIMELINE

January 2000
United beat South American champions Palmeiras to become the first British team ever to win the Intercontinental Cup.

April 2000
United relinquish their European crown, losing 3–2 on aggregate to Real Madrid.

May 2000
United retain the Premiership title, finishing with 91 points and finishing a massive 18 points clear of second-placed Arsenal.

138   MANCHESTER UNITED **OFFICIAL MEMBERS' HISTORY BOOK**

West Ham. A 1–0 home defeat to Arsenal in May signalled the end of United's league title hopes. The Reds finished a disappointing third, behind champions Arsenal and second-placed Liverpool.

The FA Cup proved elusive once more. In January 2002, an exhilarating comeback from two goals down to beat Aston Villa 3–2 raised hopes, but defensive sloppiness was again United's downfall as they lost 2–0 at Middlesbrough three weeks later.

The following month, Sir Alex Ferguson completed a welcome U-turn by postponing his retirement until the summer of 2005.

"There is a great future for Manchester United," the United boss said. "We still have a vibrant youth system and we have fantastic medical and coaching staff in place. It's exciting for me and I think those are the areas where we can make up more ground."

Meanwhile, in the Champions League quarter-final first leg, United triumphed 2–0 at Spanish side Deportivo La Coruña. David Beckham and Van Nistelrooy contributed goals of true class in United's most mature performance of the campaign. United won the return 3–2 on a typically atmospheric European night at Old Trafford.

However, two lacklustre semi-final performances against German side Bayer Leverkusen saw United eliminated on the away goals rule after a 2–2 home draw and a 1–1 result in Germany. Juan Sebastian Veron bore much of the blame after a disappointing first season with United, although he received ample support from skipper Roy Keane:

"I felt sorry for Seba. Cost £28 million, became the scapegoat for our season."

On a happier note, player of the season Ruud van Nistelrooy's scintillating form brought him an outstanding tally of 36 goals in 44 appearances, including a new Premiership record of scoring in eight consecutive matches.

Despite the disappointment of a trophyless

January 2001
A 3–1 win over West Ham on New Year's Day puts the Reds 11 points clear at the top of the Premiership table.

April 2001
Bayern Munich gain revenge for their '99 heartbreak, beating United 3–1 on aggregate in the Champions League quarter-final.

May 2001
United collect the Premiership trophy for the third year in a row and Teddy Sheringham is name PFA and FWA Footballer of the Year.

2001/02, Sir Alex Ferguson decided against implementing wholesale change at Old Trafford. But the United manager did invest a British record transfer fee of £29.1 million to lure Rio Ferdinand from Leeds United. Ferguson also signed Spanish World Cup goalkeeper Ricardo (£1.5 million from Real Valladolid).

United made a cautious start to the league campaign, defeating West Bromwich Albion 1–0 at Old Trafford and drawing 2–2 at Chelsea, where Ryan Giggs scored the 100th goal of his United career. The Reds' form was patchy thereafter with five wins, three draws and two defeats in the following 10 games.

However, the first Manchester derby of the campaign proved a watershed for United's season. A humiliating 3–1 defeat to Manchester City in November 2002 sparked the Reds into life.

"We will address the situation on the training ground," Sir Alex Ferguson promised. "We will get a reaction from this."

And what a reaction! United claimed four wins and a draw from the next five games, including the 2–0 home victory over Arsenal in early December. After a Christmas blip, United embarked on a thrilling run that saw their relentless pursuit of early pacesetters Arsenal rewarded with an eighth championship in 11 seasons.

The high points of the run-in were the 4–0 thrashing of Liverpool at Old Trafford in April 2003 and the 6–2 victory at Newcastle United five days later. United finished the season five points ahead of Arsenal, a memorable feat considering the Gunners had enjoyed a six-point lead in early February.

"There was a time when we wondered whether it might be slipping away," Rio Ferdinand admitted. "But everyone showed tremendous will to win and spirit."

The prolific form of Ruud van Nistelrooy was the key to United's success. The Dutchman set a new club record by scoring in 10 consecutive games as he notched 44 goals in 50 appearances across all competitions.

Unfortunately, the killer instinct United displayed in the Premiership was not in evidence in cup competition. After racking up 10 goals in the ties against Portsmouth and West Ham United at Old Trafford in January, United suffered the ignominy of a 2–0 FA Cup exit at home to Arsenal in mid-February.

An inability to cope with the demands of knockout competition was again United's undoing in Europe. Real Madrid dominated the first leg of a mouth-watering quarter-final, inflicting a 3–1 defeat on United. And although the Reds responded with a 4–3 victory in the return match at Old Trafford, they never controlled the tie.

July 2001
A year previously, a knee injury prevented him joining, but on 1 July 2001 Ruud van Nistelrooy finally joined United for £19 million.

February 2002
Great news as Sir Alex Ferguson announces that his retirement is postponed until summer 2005.

April 2002
Huge disappointment as United lose on away goals to Bayer Leverkusen in the Champions League semi-finals.

At least John O'Shea offered a glimpse of a bright future. The young Irish defender captured the fans' imagination with his composure and skill – including a nutmeg on Madrid's Luis Figo – throughout his first full season in the side

But David Beckham was left on the bench for the second leg of the Madrid clash amid rumours he would join the Spanish aristocrats at the end of the season. In June 2003, Beckham was transferred to Real Madrid for £25 million, thus ending a 12-year association with Old Trafford.

The summer of 2003 was a busy one at Old Trafford. Following Beckham's departure, Juan Sebastian Veron was sold to Chelsea for £15 million. And the arrival of five new players all under 24, including Tim Howard (£2.5 million from New York/New Jersey MetroStars) and Cristiano Ronaldo (£12 million from Sporting Lisbon), suggested a period of transition.

But United hit the ground running in the Premiership and their impressive early-season form included a 2–1 victory at Newcastle in August and a Van Nistelrooy-inspired 4–1 success at Leicester City the week after an infamously ugly goalless draw with Arsenal in late September.

Although there was little to choose between United, Arsenal and Chelsea at the turn of the

---

May 2002
United finish third in the league. Ruud van Nistelrooy ends his first season with 36 goals in 44 appearances.

July 2002
Rio Ferdinand signs for United for a British record transfer fee of £29.1 million.

November 2002
United suffer a shocking 3–1 derby defeat by Manchester City.

year, worryingly the Reds had already suffered three Premiership defeats. And their fourth reverse, a 1–0 defeat at Wolverhampton Wanderers in mid-January, marked the end of Rio Ferdinand's season. The England defender was banned for eight months by the FA for missing a routine drugs test in the autumn.

Without their defensive linchpin, United's league form slumped as they took just 12 points from a possible 27 in nine matches after the Wolves defeat.

Striker Louis Saha was drafted in (£13 million from Fulham) and contributed five goals in his first five league appearances. But it was not enough to help United catch leaders Arsenal, who opened up a 12-point gap before the end of March. United even found themselves seven points adrift of second-placed Chelsea. (Ultimately they would finish in third position on 75 points, four points behind Claudio Ranieri's team and a full 15 points adrift of unbeaten Arsenal).

To make matters worse, United crashed out of the Champions League after a 3–2 aggregate defeat to Portuguese champions Porto. So the only hope of a trophy lay in the FA Cup. After victories over Aston Villa, Northampton Town, Manchester City and Fulham, United faced Arsenal in the semi-finals.

With Arsenal marching relentlessly towards the league title and their hopes of a Treble still alive, United were clear underdogs going into the match at Villa Park. Arsene Wenger surprisingly omitted Thierry Henry from his starting XI, but that encouraging news was tempered by Ruud van Nistelrooy's enforced absence through injury.

After some early threats to United's goal, the difference between the two teams was clear – Arsenal desperately wanted to win, but United simply had to. Roared on by 17,000 Reds inside Villa Park, the white-shirted United heroes exhibited unbridled passion and desire

as they successfully broke up Arsenal's usual sweet passing game. Cristiano Ronaldo and Wes Brown were outstanding, but every player contributed significantly to a 1–0 win, courtesy of Paul Scholes 32nd minute goal. Arsenal's hopes of emulating United's '99 Treble triumph were dashed.

United's final opponents would be First Division Millwall, who had yet to play a Premiership side in the competition. On paper, victory looked a formality, but after some fairly dismal performances in end-of-season Premiership games (including 1–0 defeats by Portsmouth, Blackburn and Liverpool), United fans and players alike were wary of over-confidence. At the Millennium Stadium in Cardiff, the Lions battled valiantly, but a header by Cristiano Ronaldo just before half-time broke their resistance and a 65th minute penalty and tap-in on 81 minutes by Ruud van Nistelrooy secured a 3–0 win and extended the club's FA Cup-winning record to 11.

So, 2003/04 ended with another trophy in the Old Trafford cabinet, and although it had been a relatively difficult campaign, there had been some pluses to enjoy. Ruud van Nistelrooy bagged his 100th and 101st goals during the 4–3 Premiership victory at Everton in February, in just his 131st United

![Louis Saha]

appearance. Of the new recruits, Tim Howard proved the most consistent, replacing Fabien Barthez, who was released from his Old Trafford contract, while Cristiano Ronaldo and Darren Fletcher served notice of their immense natural talent.

Continuity was also ensured when Sir Alex Ferguson agreed a new 12-month rolling contract which will start in June 2005 when his present contract runs out. "It gives me strong focus on the short-term challenges in the new season ahead as well as the long-term freedom to look to improve our current squad", commented a happy Ferguson. The Reds go marching on.

A disappointing 2003/04 season overall ended on a high note with a 3–0 victory in the FA Cup Final over Millwall.

January 2004
Louis Saha signs; Rio Ferdinand begins an eight-month ban for missing a drugs test. Subsequently, United's league form slumps dramatically.

April 2004
A month after Porto knock United out of the Champions League, the Reds beat Arsenal 1–0 in the FA Cup semi-final.

May 2004
After finishing a disappointing third place in the Premiership, United gain some consolation with a 3–0 FA Cup final win over Millwall